HOSEA
and
JOEL

J. Vernon McGee

THOMAS NELSON PUBLISHERS

Nashville • Atlanta • London • Vancouver

Published in Nashville, Tennessee, by Thomas Nelson, Inc.

Scripture quotations are from the KING JAMES VERSION of the Bible.

Library of Congress Cataloging-in-Publication Data

McGee, J. Vernon (John Vernon), 1904–1988
    [Thru the Bible with J. Vernon McGee]
    Thru the Bible commentary series / J. Vernon McGee.
      p.   cm.
    Reprint. Originally published: Thru the Bible with J. Vernon McGee. 1975.
    Includes bibliographical references.
    ISBN 0-7852-1029-6 (TR)
    ISBN 0-7852-1088-1 (NRM)
    1. Bible—Commentaries. I. Title.
BS491.2.M37 1991
220.7′7—dc20   90–41340
                                 CIP

PRINTED IN MEXICO
10 11 12 13 – 03 02

CONTENTS

HOSEA

JOEL

PREFACE

The radio broadcasts of the Thru the Bible Radio five-year program were transcribed, edited, and published first in single-volume paperbacks to accommodate the radio audience.

There has been a minimal amount of further editing for this publication. Therefore, these messages are not the word-for-word recording of the taped messages which went out over the air. The changes were necessary to accommodate a reading audience rather than a listening audience.

These are popular messages, prepared originally for a radio audience. They should not be considered a commentary on the entire Bible in any sense of that term. These messages are devoid of any attempt to present a theological or technical commentary on the Bible. Behind these messages is a great deal of research and study in order to interpret the Bible from a popular rather than from a scholarly (and too-often boring) viewpoint.

We have definitely and deliberately attempted "to put the cookies on the bottom shelf so that the kiddies could get them."

The fact that these messages have been translated into many languages for radio broadcasting and have been received with enthusiasm reveals the need for a simple teaching of the whole Bible for the masses of the world.

I am indebted to many people and to many sources for bringing this volume into existence. I should express my especial thanks to my secretary, Gertrude Cutler, who supervised the editorial work; to Dr. Elliott R. Cole, my associate, who handled all the detailed work with the publishers; and finally, to my wife Ruth for tenaciously encouraging me from the beginning to put my notes and messages into printed form.

Solomon wrote, ". . . of making many books there is no end; and much study is a weariness of the flesh" (Eccl. 12:12). On a sea of books that flood the marketplace, we launch this series of THRU THE BIBLE with the hope that it might draw many to the one Book, *The Bible.*

J. VERNON McGEE

HOSEA

The Book of
HOSEA

INTRODUCTION

Beginning with Hosea and concluding with Malachi, there are twelve short prophecies designated as the Minor Prophets, while Isaiah, Jeremiah, Ezekiel, and Daniel are called the Major Prophets. The Minor Prophets are so called because of the size of the books, not because of their content. However, even that criterion for division is not completely accurate since Hosea is a longer book than Daniel. Actually, the so-called Minor Prophets are not minor. Each of them batted in the major league and was a star in the message that he brought.

The Minor Prophets were exceedingly nationalistic, but they were not isolationists. They dealt with the fact that God's people had broken the law of God, the Ten Commandments. This necessarily puts an emphasis on works, good works. For this reason the liberals and the promoters of the social gospel have used the Minor Prophets a great deal. Unfortunately, they have missed the main message of these prophets. We will see some of that when we get into the prophecy of Hosea. The Minor Prophets warned against godless alliances with other nations. They were extremely patriotic and denounced political and moral corruption. They warned Israel against an isolationism from God.

Hosea lived during the time of the divided kingdom. He was a prophet to the northern kingdom which is called the kingdom of Israel, distinguished from the southern kingdom known as the kingdom of Judah. "The word of the LORD that came unto Hosea, the son of Beeri, in the days of Uzziah, Jotham, Ahaz, and Hezekiah, kings of

Judah, and in the days of Jeroboam the son of Joash, king of Israel" (Hos. 1:1).

Hosea mentions the four kings of Judah first, and then he mentions the king of Israel, the northern kingdom. Because they were all contemporary with Hosea, he mentions them all. He was a prophet to the northern kingdom of Israel, as the content of the book reveals.

Hosea was a contemporary of Amos, another prophet to Israel. He was also a contemporary of Micah and Isaiah, prophets to Judah. His ministry extended over half a century, and he lived to see the fulfillment of his prophecy in the captivity of Israel.

He can be compared to Jeremiah in the southern kingdom. Jeremiah warned his people of the southern kingdom that they would go into captivity, and he lived to see it. Hosea warned the northern kingdom that they would be going into Assyrian captivity, and he lived to see it. Jeremiah and Hosea have a great many things in common.

The theme of this book is a plea to return unto the Lord. I have a message entitled, "The Greatest Sin in All the World," which emphasizes the great theme of this book. I shall let it serve as the introduction to this marvelous prophecy of Hosea.

The accusation is often made that the present-day pulpit is weak and uncertain. Furthermore, it is charged that instead of being a ". . . voice . . . in the wilderness . . ." (John 1:23), the modern pulpit has settled down comfortably to become a sounding board for the whims and wishes of an indifferent people with itching ears. If the charge is true (and in many cases it is), it is because the pulpit is reluctant to grapple with the great issues of life. This hesitancy is born of a desire to escape criticism and a dread of becoming offensive to the finer sensibilities. More often it is due to a cowardly fear of facing the raw realities of life and wrestling with the leviathan of living issues. The pulpit quotes poetry and sprinkles rose water. It lives in a land of make-believe instead of saying, "Believe on the Lord Jesus Christ, and thou shalt be saved . . ." (Acts 16:31).

The theater, the monthly magazine, and other agencies of communication deal with life stripped of its niceties. These instruments for reaching and teaching the masses take the gloves off and grapple with the problems that we face daily.

Not so the pulpit. The pulpit has avoided these issues. As we come to this prophecy of Hosea, we cannot avoid dealing with the problems and issues of life, for that is the story that is behind the headlines in the prophecy of Hosea. It is not a pretty story, but we must understand it if we are to understand the message of Hosea.

The story behind the prophecy of Hosea is the tragedy of a broken home. The personal experience of Hosea is the background of his message. He walks out of a broken home to speak to the nation from a heart that is breaking. He knew exactly how *God* felt, because *he* felt the same way.

The home is the rock foundation of society and has been that for all peoples. God has given the home to mankind. He gave it to man at the very beginning. It is the most important unit in the social structure. It is to society what the atom is to the physical universe. The little atom has been called the building block of the universe. Well, the home is the building block of society. The character and color of a building is determined by the individual bricks that go into it. No nation is any stronger than the homes that populate it, for the home determines the color and complexion of society. The home is the chain of a nation that holds it together, and every individual link is important.

Home is where we live and move and have our being. It is in the home where we are ourselves. We dress up physically and psychologically when we go out. We put up quite a front when we go through our front door and move out upon the street. But it is within the walls of the home that we take off our masks and are really ourselves.

Because of the strategic position of the home, God has thrown about it certain safeguards to protect it. He has surrounded it with certain bulwarks because of its importance. One of these is marriage. God has given more attention to the institution of marriage than He has to any other institution in this world. Society did not *make* marriage; society *found* marriage. It is God who made marriage, and He gave it to mankind. Marriage rests upon His direct Word, ". . . What therefore God hath joined together, let not man put asunder" (Matt. 19:6). God performed the first marriage ceremony. He gave the first bride away. He blessed the first couple. Marriage is more than a legal contract, more than an economic arrangement, more than a union of those with mutual love; it is an act of God. It rests upon His fiat command. Many folk think that all they need in order to get married is a license and a preacher. My friend, if you are going to have a successful marriage, you have to have God. If God does not make the marriage, it will go on the rocks.

God has given a drive to the race to reproduce within the framework of marriage. That is what makes the home. The ". . . twain shall be one flesh . . ." (Mark 10:8). Before man walked out of the Garden of Eden, God gave him this institution. Besides the skins that Adam and Eve wore, the only thing they had was a marriage certificate from God. That is all. That is the only institution that came out of the Garden of Eden.

Marriage is a sacred relationship; it is a holy union. The New Testament sums up the mind of God on this when it says, "Marriage is honourable in all . . ." (Heb. 13:4). Therefore, my beloved, marriage cannot be broken by a little legal act. It cannot be broken by a fit of temper. It cannot be broken by self-will. I personally believe there are only two acts that break a marriage—I mean a *real* marriage.

The first act is death, of course, which automatically severs the relationship.

The second act is unfaithfulness—unfaithfulness on the part of either the husband or the wife. That rips a relationship in two. In the Old Testament, the one guilty of adultery was to be dealt with in the harshest manner imaginable. For example, notice the importance God attached to the act: "And the man that committeth adultery with another man's wife, even he that committeth adultery with his neighbour's wife, the adulterer and the adulteress shall surely be put to death" (Lev. 20:10). For an unmarried girl accused of adultery the Law said, "But if this thing be true, and the tokens of virginity be not found for the damsel: then they shall bring out the damsel to the door of her father's house, and the men of her city shall stone her with stones that she die: because she hath wrought folly in Israel, to play the whore in her father's house: so shalt thou put evil away from among you" (Deut. 22:20–21).

There are a few words I think we should say here by way of explanation. There are some zealous Christians who use Romans 7:2–3 as the basis for the extreme viewpoint that a divorced person who has a living mate can never remarry. Verse 2 says, "For the woman which hath an husband is bound by the law to her husband so long as he liveth; but if the husband be dead, she is loosed from the law of her husband." They forget that under the Law the married person who was guilty of fornication was stoned to death and the innocent party under the Law did not have a living partner. The guilty person was pushing up daisies through the rock pile. If that were enforced in Southern California today, we wouldn't have freeways because we wouldn't be able to get around all the rock piles.

I am not sure but what Paul includes desertion under the heading of unfaithfulness in 1 Corinthians 7:15: "But if the unbelieving depart, let him depart. A brother or a sister is not under bondage in such cases: but God hath called us to peace."

Another item concerning the Law which needs amplification is the reference in Deuteronomy which seems to preclude the man from any charge of guilt. You may wonder why the woman is picked on—isn't the man guilty? Yes, but there are two things you need to bear in mind: one is that the word used is always the generic term, *anthropōs*, meaning "mankind." We have the same distinction in legal terminology. I notice that some contracts read, "The party of the first part, if he . . ." when the person is really a she. The term is used for either one. Also we must remember that marriage is a picture of Christ and the church, and He is never guilty, but the church is guilty. The Scriptures do not teach a double standard, but I do think they teach a different standard.

Personally, I think that God has made woman finer than man. For this reason, when she goes bad, she goes farther down than a man goes. It is not that sin in one is worse than in another, but the results are far more detrimental. In my limited ministry, I have seen children overcome the handicap of a ne'er-do-well father, but I have never seen children turn out right when the mother has been bad. A sorry father is a serious handicap for a child, but a good mother more than compensates. Mother is the center of the home. Some time ago I heard of a woman who was asked to accept an office in a church organization. She refused the office and gave as her reason, "I am a missionary to the nursery. There are three pairs of eyes watching me, and I want to direct them to God." God has placed a mother in a home and made her all-important in that place.

Every woman was once a little girl very much like the description composed by Alan Beck, and which he has entitled "What is a Girl?"

Little girls are the nicest things that happen to people. They are born with a little bit of angel-shine about them and though it wears thin sometimes, there is always enough left to lasso your heart—even when they are sitting in the mud, or crying temperamental tears, or parading up the street in mother's best clothes.

A little girl can be sweeter (and badder) oftener than anyone else in the world. She can jitter around, and stomp, and make funny noises and frazzle your nerves, yet just when you open your mouth, she stands there demure with that special look in her eyes. A girl is Innocence playing in the mud, Beauty standing on its head, and Motherhood dragging a doll by the foot.

God borrows from many creatures to make a little girl. He uses the song of a bird, the squeal of a pig, the stubbornness of a mule, the antics of a monkey, the spryness of a grasshopper, the curiosity of a cat, the slyness of a fox, the softness of a kitten. And to top it off, He adds the mysterious mind of a woman.

A little girl likes new shoes, party dresses, small animals, dolls, make-believe, ice cream, make-up, going visiting, tea parties, and one boy. She doesn't care so much for visitors, boys in general, large dogs, hand-me-downs, straight chairs, vegetables, snow suits, or staying in the front yard. She is loudest when you are thinking, prettiest when she has provoked you, busiest at bedtime, quietest when you want to show her off, and most flirtatious when she absolutely must not get the best of you again.

She can muss up your home, your hair, and your dignity—spend your money, your time, and your temper—then just when your patience is ready to crack, her sunshine peeks through and you're lost again.

Yes, she is a nerve-racking nuisance, just a noisy bundle of mischief. But when your dreams tumble down and the world is a mess, when it seems you are pretty much of a fool after all, she can make you a king when she climbs on your knee and whispers, "I love you best of all!"

God shapes that little-girl charm into a fine and delicate instrument, a woman. But when a woman goes wrong, the tragedy is immeasurable.

The background of the prophecy of Hosea is the story of a fallen woman and a broken home. It is a story of that which must be contrasted to God's ideal of marriage and of womanhood. God uses this to tell His own story.

In the hill country of Ephraim, in one of the many little towns not on the maps of the world, lived two young people. One was a boy by the name of Hosea, the other was a girl by the name of Gomer. They fell in love—it is the same story which has been repeated millions of times but never grows old. I don't think it is stretching the imagination to say that they fell madly in love with each other. Then for some unaccountable reason, Gomer went bad. She resorted to the oldest profession known to mankind. Hosea was brokenhearted, and shame filled his soul. He must have thought about his recourse to the Mosaic Law. He could have brought her before the elders of the town and demanded the law be enforced. In that case she would have been stoned, for she had betrayed him. He would have been justified.

Does this remind you of another story that took place some seven hundred years later in that same hill country when a man by the name of Joseph was engaged to a girl by the name of Mary? The principal difference is that Joseph's information was wrong, and an angel came from heaven to correct it; but Hosea's information was right, for Gomer was guilty.

At this particular juncture the Book of Hosea opens. "The beginning of the word of the LORD by Hosea. And the LORD said to Hosea, Go, take unto thee a wife of whoredoms and children of whoredoms: for the land hath committed great whoredom, departing from the LORD" (Hos. 1:2). There are expositors who take the position that this is nothing but an allegory, that it did not really happen. Such trifling with the Word of God waters it down to a harmless solution which is more sickening than stimulating. Let's face it—God commanded Hosea to break the Mosaic Law. The Law said to stone her, but God said to marry her. The thing God commanded Hosea to do must have caused him to revolt in every fiber of his being, but Hosea did not demur—he obeyed explicitly. He took Gomer in holy wedlock, and he gave her his name. She came into his home as his wife. Listen to the apostle Paul as he speaks of such a relationship: "What? know ye not that he which is joined to an harlot is one body? for two, saith he, shall be one flesh" (1 Cor. 6:16).

My friend, you may be sure that the tempo of gossip really picked up in that little town. Hosea's home became a desert island in a sea of criticism. It was the isolation ward in local society. A case of leprosy in the home would not have broken off contact with the outside world more effectively. Poor Hosea!

Children were born in this home. There were three—two boys and one girl. Their names, in their meanings, tell the awful story. And there is the larger meaning and message for the nation Israel.

Jezreel was the oldest. His name means "God will scatter, and God will avenge." The reference, God told Hosea, was directly to the house of Jehu. Although Jehu had carried out God's instructions to destroy the house of Ahab, he had done it with hatred and great personal vengeance. For this, God says, "I'll judge. I'll scatter Israel, but there will be mercy in My judgment."

The second child was Lo-ruhamah, which means that she never knew a father's pity. It was not that she was an orphan, but she did not know who her father was. What a scandal in the home of Hosea! God is saying through this circumstance to the people of the northern kingdom who had gone into idolatry, "You will not know My pity, for I am not your Father."

The third child was Lo-ammi—which means "not my people." If you put this in the singular, it would mean "not my child." What a message that was to Hosea's day! And what a message it is to our own day when liberal theology claims that everyone is a child of God. God says they are wrong. He has no illegitimate children. God says, "I know who My children are. Do you think that My children are the offspring of a man-made union? Absolutely not! A person becomes My child only through faith in Jesus Christ." And the Lord Jesus said to the men in His day who claimed to be the sons of Abraham, "Ye are of your father the *devil* . . ." (John 8:44, italics mine). They could make no claim of being God's children.

My friend, are you Lo-ammi? Are you God's child, or are you an illegitimate child? Let me assure you that you can become a child of God—"But as many as received him, to them gave he power [the right, the authority] to become the sons of God, even to them that believe on his name" (John 1:12).

The story of Hosea's home is a sad one, and the story continues. Gomer left home. She returned to her former profession and became a common prostitute. Certainly God is going to say to this man, "Hosea, you have done all that you can. You tried to reform the woman, but it didn't do any good. Let her go." But no, God says, "Go get her and bring her back to your home." Hosea went after her. She refused to come back. He sent the children to plead with their mother. Still she would not return. Then, as women of this sort did in those days, she sold herself into slavery. Hosea went to her and *bought* her and brought her back to the home.

Oh, my friend, what a picture this is of our Savior. He created us and we belong to Him. Then we were guilty of going from Him and giving our love, our affection, our time, to the things of the world. And while we were yet sinners, He came down to this earth and *bought* us in our ugly condition that He might make us His legitimate children. What love!

After this experience, did Gomer become a faithful wife? The record does not tell us. But we see Hosea, stepping out of a home scarred by shame and going before a nation with a heart that is breaking. His sorrow is intolerable; with scalding tears coursing down his cheeks, he denounces the nation Israel, saying, "You have been faithless to God! I know how God feels, because I feel the same way. You have broken the heart of God." What a picture!

Hosea denounced the nation. He declared a verdict of guilty for the crime of all crimes. He said simply but specifically that their sin was as black as it could be and they could expect God's punishment. This people who had known God, whom He had redeemed out of Egypt, to whom He had said, "Ye have seen what I did unto the Egyptians, and how I bare you on eagles' wings, and brought you unto myself" (Exod. 19:4), turned their backs on God and made a golden calf! And still in Hosea's day they had not learned their lesson, for at that moment in the northern kingdom there stood two golden calves. The people had turned from the living and true God back to calf worship! Israel was playing the harlot. Their sin was the greatest sin in the world.

You may be saying, "I thought unbelief was the greatest sin." In one sense unbelief is the greatest sin, but it is not an act, it is a state. We all are born in rebellion against God. But, thank God, Christ's death paid the penalty for our sin, and if you and I exercise faith in Jesus Christ, He will save us. It is true that unbelief is a terrible sin for which there is but one remedy—the remedy is to trust Christ. When you continue in unbelief, you reject the remedy.

There is another sin which you may consider the greatest in the world: it is sin against light. To have the light of the gospel of Jesus Christ and reject it is sinning against light. Frankly, I would rather stand before God's throne of judgment as an idolater from the darkest jungle of Africa, than as a church member who has repeatedly heard the gospel and rejected it. But this is not the greatest sin.

The greatest sin in all the world is sin against love. This is worse than all others, and this is the message of Hosea. Gomer was not only guilty of breaking the marriage vow, which was bad enough, but she sinned against the one who loved her. That is sin at its worst. My friend, to sin against God and the Savior who loves you is worse than the animism and animalism of the heathen world. The sin of paganism is nothing compared to the sin of those who reject God's love. It is deeper and darker than the immorality of the underworld and the demonism of the overworld.

Hosea knew what sin was, and he knew what love was. Sin against love makes the sin more heinous.

Israel knew the love of God as no other nation knew it. She knew His deliverance, His redemption, His protection, His forgiveness, His revelation, and His love. Yet Israel turned to dumb idols and gave herself to them. This is sin at its worst.

However, God would not give her up. Love will triumph. Let me lift out just three verses from Hosea's prophecy which will tell God's story:

First, here is the charge: "Ephraim is joined to idols: let him alone" (Hos. 4:17). The name *Ephraim* is synonymous with the name *Israel*, and He charges Israel with spiritual adultery.

Then notice the great pulsating passion of the infinite God: "How shall I give thee up, Ephraim? how shall I deliver thee, Israel? how shall I make thee as Admah? how shall I set thee as Zeboim? mine heart is turned within me, my repentings are kindled together" (Hos. 11:8). God is saying that He can't give Israel up; He loves her too much. This is His reason for sending Hosea back to get Gomer a second and a third time. He wanted Hosea to know how He felt about Israel.

Finally, here is the victory: "Ephraim shall say, What have I to do any more with idols? I have heard him, and observed him: I am like a green fir tree. From me is thy fruit found" (Hos. 14:8). There is a day coming when Israel will turn back to God. This leads us to believe that Gomer finally did change and become a good wife and mother. We cannot be sure of this, but we can be sure that Israel will one day return to God with her whole heart.

Is there an application for you and me here? Does this shocking description of spiritual adultery fit the believer in our day? Yes, the church is described as the bride of Christ—". . . I have espoused you . . . that I may present you as a chaste virgin to Christ" (2 Cor. 11:2). And to the church at Ephesus the Lord Jesus said, "I know thy works, and thy labour, and thy patience, and how thou canst not bear them which are evil. . . . Nevertheless I have somewhat against thee, because thou hast left thy first love" (Rev. 2:2, 4).

My friend, it is not enough to be correct in your doctrine and be active in your service for Christ. These are important and have their place, but the essential thing is love. Have you left your first love? Do you *love* Him today?

The name *Hosea* means "salvation"; it is another form of *Joshua*, which is the Hebrew name of the Greek form *Jesus*. The church is the bride of the New Testament Hosea, but our Hosea is joined to a spiritual harlot!

In Revelation, chapter 17, is the most frightful picture in the Bible. It personifies the church and calls her the great harlot, Mystery Babylon. This is the trend which the organized church is following in our day. Oh, how many believers are covering up their frustration and their lack of reality in their spiritual experience by just being busy. It is nothing in the world but nervous agitation. Down underneath they cannot honestly say, "I love Him. I am true to Him." With hot tears our Lord accuses the church of being lukewarm. God pity the man who is married to a lukewarm woman. God pity our Savior who is joined to a church that is only lukewarm. He says, "Oh, how I wish that you were either hot or cold!"

Let me be very personal and ask about *your* relationship with Christ. Has any cloud come between your soul and your Savior? An incident is told of Spurgeon who suddenly stopped in the middle of the street he was crossing and prayed. When he reached the other side, his companion asked him, "Why did you stop to pray in the middle of the street?" Spurgeon's reply was something like this, "A cloud came between my soul and Christ, and I could not let it remain there even long enough to reach the other side of the street." Before the Lord Jesus put Simon Peter in harness, He asked the heart-searching question, ". . . Lovest thou me? . . ." (John 21:17). This is just as poignant and pertinent now as it was that early dawn by the Sea of Galilee.

My friend, when you turn your back on the One who so loved the world that He gave His only begotten Son, you are not only doing something bad, you are not merely turning away in unbelief, you are committing the greatest sin of all. You are turning away from a God who loves you and died for you. There is no other sin equal to that.

OUTLINE

I. **Personal—The Prophet and His Faithless Wife, Gomer, Chapters 1—3**
  A. Marriage of Hosea and Gomer, the Harlot, Chapter 1
  B. Gomer Proves Faithless; Israel Proves Faithless; God Proves Faithful, Chapter 2
  C. Hosea Commanded to Take Gomer Again, Chapter 3

II. **Prophetic—The Lord and the Faithless Nation Israel, Chapters 4—14**
  A. Israel Plays the Harlot, Chapters 4—5
    1. Israel Guilty of Lawlessness, Immorality, Ignorance of God's Word, and Idolatry, Chapter 4
    2. Israel Turns from God; God Turns from Israel; Deterioration within Follows, Chapter 5
  B. Israel (Ephraim) Will Return in the Last Days; Presently to Be Judged for Current Sins, Chapter 6
  C. Israel (Ephraim) Could Escape Judgment by Turning to God Who Loves Her (Key: 11:8), Chapters 7—12
    1. Israel (Silly Dove) Turns to Egypt and Assyria, Chapter 7
    2. Israel Turns to Golden Calves and Altars of Sin, Chapter 8
    3. Israel (Backsliding Heifer) Turns to Land Productivity; Will Be Driven from Land, Chapters 9—10
    4. Israel Turns from God—Must Be Judged; God Will Not Give Up on Her, Chapters 11—12
  D. Israel (Ephraim) Will Turn from Idols to God in Last Days, Chapters 13—14
    1. Israel Will Be Judged in the Present, Chapter 13
    2. Israel Will Be Saved in the Future, Chapter 14

CHAPTER 1

THEME: The marriage of Hosea and Gomer, the harlot

W hen we come to the prophecy of Hosea, we are coming to one of the great books of the Bible and to a man who was a remarkable prophet. I personally do not like the classification of the prophets as Major and Minor. Every one of these men, whether they wrote a long prophecy or not, was an outstanding man. You wouldn't call Elijah a minor prophet simply because he never wrote a prophecy, would you? And John the Baptist, the last of the prophets, never wrote anything; yet he was a prophet of God and announced the coming of the Savior.

The prophets were not grouped as Major and Minor in the Hebrew Bible. They were arranged as we have them by the church around the third century. If I could have had my way in the arrangement of the books of the Bible, I would have placed each prophet with the historical book to which it corresponds. You will notice that the messages of nearly all the writing prophets belong to the period of the divided kingdom. When the kings failed, God then raised up prophets to speak to the nation.

Chronologically, therefore, the prophecy of Hosea belongs before Jeremiah. Hosea was contemporary with Isaiah, Micah, and his compatriot, Amos, in the northern kingdom. Hosea and Amos were prophets in the northern kingdom, Isaiah and Micah in the southern kingdom.

Hosea compares in many respects to Jeremiah. Jeremiah was the last prophet before the southern kingdom went into captivity; but more than a hundred years before that, Hosea was a prophet in the northern kingdom. He, like Jeremiah, warned the nation of its impending captivity. Both men spoke out of a heartbreaking personal experience, although Jeremiah's was more public. Hosea's experience was in the home while Jeremiah's was in the nation. Jeremiah loved his nation, and it broke his heart to give them such a harsh message, but God chose a very tenderhearted man for the job. Perhaps Hosea was not as tenderhearted as Jeremiah, but we will see that he came from the experience of a broken home with a broken heart. His wife was unfaithful to him and became a harlot. He loved her so much that he went back and took her again. And again she played the harlot. Coming from this experience, this man walked out before the nation Israel, with hot tears streaming down his cheeks, and said, "I want to tell you how God feels about you, because I feel the same way. I have had a personal experience in my own home." Because this man's heart had been broken, he could speak God's message to his nation.

In the first three chapters of Hosea we have that which is *personal*, the story of the prophet and his faithless wife, Gomer. We have here the scandal of his home and the gossip of the town.

THE MARRIAGE OF HOSEA AND GOMER, THE HARLOT

The word of the LORD that came unto Hosea, the son of Beeri, in the days of Uzziah, Jotham, Ahaz, and Hezekiah, kings of Judah, and in the days of Jeroboam the son of Joash, king of Israel [Hos. 1:1].

"Uzziah, Jotham, Ahaz, and Hezekiah, kings of Judah"—these were the kings in the south at this particular time.

"Jereboam the son of Joash, king of Israel"—there couldn't have been a worse king than this king of the northern kingdom.

The beginning of the word of the LORD by Hosea. And the LORD said to Hosea, Go, take unto thee a wife of whoredoms and children of whoredoms: for the land hath committed great whoredom, departing from the LORD [Hos. 1:2].

What the Lord says to the prophet is a rather startling thing, and many interpreters do not take Him literally. I highly recommend *The Scofield Reference Bible*, and I use the older edition a great deal. Some folk feel that those of us who recommend this Bible believe its notes are inspired. I do not believe they are inspired, and the first note given for this verse in *The New Scofield Reference Bible* is one that I totally disagree with. It reads: "God did not command Hosea to take an immoral wife but permitted him to carry out his desire to marry Gomer, warning him that she would be unfaithful, and using the prophet's sad experience as a basis for the presentation of lessons about God's relation to Israel." I consider this a very nice way to get God off the hook, but you do not have to get Him off the hook—he takes full responsibility for this.

The way that I understand this verse is that God said to Hosea, "Go." When my parents said that to me as a boy—"*Go* to the store," or "*Go* to school"—I always interpreted that as a command. When God said to Hosea, "Go," He was not just granting him permission to marry Gomer; it was a *command* to do so. Hosea probably was a young man, probably living in the Ephraim country of the northern kingdom. He met this beautiful girl and fell madly in love with her, and then she played the harlot. Naturally he wanted to put her aside. He might have wanted to marry her, but he wouldn't dare do that in a little town—and the Mosaic Law said to stone her. What is he going to do? God said, "Go and marry her." God is actually asking him to break the Mosaic Law. Someone will say, "That's terrible." Not when God tells you to do it, my friend. God said to him, "Hosea, you were in love with her, and now you want to put her aside. I don't want you to put her aside; I want you to marry her. She is a wife of harlotry and child of harlotry." Apparently there was a record of unfaithfulness in her family.

Here at the very beginning, the Lord makes clear to Hosea how He is going to use this experience in the prophet's life. He said, "For the land hath committed great whoredom, departing from the LORD." He is comparing that which is physical harlotry or adultery to that which is spiritual harlotry or adultery.

This is applicable to the believer today. You can play fast and loose with God, and you are nothing in the world but a harlot, a spiritual harlot, in His sight. That is exactly the language He uses here, and

God uses pretty plain language. I wish the pulpit today were a little stronger than it is. We all are trying to be very nice and, as a result, we sometimes do not speak as strongly as the Word of God does.

> **So he went and took Gomer the daughter of Diblaim; which conceived, and bare him a son.**

> **And the LORD said unto him, Call his name Jezreel; for yet a little while, and I will avenge the blood of Jezreel upon the house of Jehu, and will cause to cease the kingdom of the house of Israel.**

> **And it shall come to pass at that day, that I will break the bow of Israel in the valley of Jezreel [Hos. 1:3–5].**

Not only the marriage but also the children are going to present a real spiritual lesson for the nation Israel. (Remember that Isaiah's children also had a spiritual message for the nation.) Jezreel is the name of the son; it means "God will scatter." God says, "I will avenge the blood of Jezreel." Jezreel is the name of a city and also of a famous plain, the plain of Armageddon, or the Valley of Esdraelon. It has a long, bloody history and will have a similar future as the place where the last war will end. God is saying here that He is going to scatter the northern kingdom.

> **And she conceived again, and bare a daughter. And God said unto him, Call her name Lo-ruhamah: for I will no more have mercy upon the house of Israel; but I will utterly take them away [Hos. 1:6].**

God named her Lo-ruhamah, which means that she "never knew a father's pity." As I indicated previously, it was not that she was an orphan, but she did not know who her father was. This reveals the scandal in the home of Hosea! God is saying through this circumstance to the people of the northern kingdom who had gone into idolatry, "You will not know My pity, for I am not your Father."

There has always been the question as to the possibility of a person stepping over a line—that is, sinking so low in sin that the grace of God cannot reach him. While I do not believe that you could ever get to a place where God by His grace *could* not save you, I do believe that if you persist in rejecting God's grace and mercy, the day will come when you will step over that line. This does not mean the grace of God cannot reach you, but it does mean that there will be nothing in you that the grace of God can lay hold of.

Let me illustrate this with the story of a man I met when I first came to Pasadena, California, as a pastor in 1940. His wife wanted me to visit him in his home because he was sick and dying. She asked me to present the gospel to him, and I did. He was a very polite man, and he listened to me. Then he said, "I would say, 'Yes, I will accept Christ as my Savior'—in fact, I am going to do it. But I want to tell you this: I have played and trifled with God all my life. I have been down to an altar twenty-five times. I have made promises to Him and then turned from Him, and I have never been sincere. Honestly, I cannot tell you right now whether I am sincere or not." All I could do at his funeral as I looked down at him was to say under my breath, "Oh, God, I hope he was sincere. I hope he really meant it. I hope Your grace reached down and touched him."

You *can* trifle with God too long. The nation Israel did, and the day came when God said, "I will no longer have mercy on you."

But I will have mercy upon the house of Judah, and will save them by the Lord their God, and will not save them by bow, nor by sword, nor by battle, by horses, nor by horsemen [Hos. 1:7].

"However," God said, "I am not ready yet to judge the house of *Judah*." Why will He spare Judah and not Israel? For the sake of David. God had said that for the sake of David He would not divide the kingdom under the rule of Solomon. Again and again He said that for the sake of David He would save the southern kingdom. Someone may want to criticize this and say that it is not fair. I don't know whether it is fair or not, but I thank God that He showed mercy to me, that He was patient and continued to show mercy. And He continues to do so even today.

"And will save them by the LORD their God, and will not save them by bow, nor by sword, nor by battle, by horses, nor by horsemen." In effect, God says, "I am not going to save them by the fact that they have phantom jets and atom bombs. I am not going to save them by the means of arms." If you read 2 Kings 19 and Isaiah 37, you will learn how God miraculously delivered the people of the southern kingdom at this time. But He did not deliver the northern kingdom.

Now when she had weaned Lo-ruhamah, she conceived, and bare a son [Hos. 1:8].

In that country they take about two to three years to wean a child. When Lo-ruhamah was weaned, Gomer had another son.

Then said God, Call his name Lo-ammi: for ye are not my people, and I will not be your God [Hos. 1:9].

The third child was *Lo-ammi*, which means "not my people." If you put this in the singular, it would mean "not my child." There was a question about the second child; there is no question about this one. And God is saying to the nation Israel, "Ye are not my people, and I will not be your God." If this were the only verse in the Bible, I would have to agree with the amillennialists who say that God is through dealing with the nation Israel. All of us—including many of my premillennial brethren—need to be very careful not to reach into the Bible and pull out a verse here or there and say that it is being fulfilled. If the entire prophecy of Hosea is read, no one can convincingly argue that God is through with the nation Israel. The next verse makes this very clear—

Yet the number of the children of Israel shall be as the sand of the sea, which cannot be measured nor numbered; and it shall come to pass, that in the place where it was said unto them, Ye are not my people, there it shall be said unto them, Ye are the sons of the living God [Hos. 1:10].

"Yet the number of the children of Israel shall be as the sand of the sea, which cannot be measured nor numbered." The Hebrew people have been decimated again and again by persecution—think of what Hitler did! Yet here is a marvelous prophecy that God is going to increase their number.

"And it shall come to pass, that in the place where it was said unto them, Ye are not my people, there it shall be said unto them, Ye are the sons of the living God." In that day there will be a great turning to God. God is not through with Israel—that is clear when you read the entire Word of God.

Then shall the children of Judah and the children of Israel be gathered together, and appoint themselves one head, and they shall come up out of the land: for great shall be the day of Jezreel [Hos. 1:11].

"Then shall the children of Judah and the children of Israel be gathered together." The nation shall come together. There are no "ten lost tribes of Israel," by the way.

"And appoint themselves one head." They don't have that today—they are not all in agreement with their leadership. The "one head" referred to in Hosea's prophecy is the Messiah, of course.

"And they shall come up out of the land: for great shall be the day of Jezreel"—what a wonderful prophecy this is. However, I disagree with the viewpoint that the present return to Israel is a fulfillment of Old Testament prophecy. We shall deal with that in greater detail as we go through the Book of Hosea.

CHAPTER 2

THEME: Gomer proves faithless; Israel proves faithless; God proves faithful

This chapter opens with the fifth very remarkable prophecy concerning the nation Israel. In the last two verses of the preceding chapter we saw that (1) Israel will experience a great increase in population; (2) in the nation there will be a great turning to God; (3) the northern and southern kingdoms will reunite so that the twelve tribes will again form a single nation; (4) they will appoint themselves one head, who will be the Messiah; and (5)—

Say ye unto your brethren, Ammi; and to your sisters, Ruhamah [Hos. 2:1].

Ammi means "my people," and *Ruhamah* means "pitied." God is saying to the nation that the day is coming when He is going to say, "You are My people." My friend, God is not through with the nation Israel, as we will see in chapter 3. This is very important to understand. Those who teach that God is through with Israel either spiritualize or discount a great deal of the Old Testament. If you can strip the Old Testament of its literal meaning, that gives you the liberty to do the same to the New Testament. Do you want to rob the Epistle of Romans and even John 3:16 of their literal meaning? You cannot do that with the New Testament, and I don't believe you can do it with the Old Testament either.

Plead with your mother, plead: for she is not my wife, neither am I her husband: let her therefore put away her whoredoms out of her sight, and her adulteries from between her breasts [Hos. 2:2].

"Plead" carries the thought of a great contention, because Israel like Gomer was unfaithful and went back to practicing prostitution. God is applying Gomer's sin to the nation. Hosea married a girl who had become a harlot, and, even after they had been married for some time and had three children, she went back to prostitution again. And all the while this man Hosea *loved* her! The greatest sin in all the world is not murder or theft or lying or possibly, under certain circumstances, adultery. But judging from what Scripture teaches, the worst sin one can commit is to become unfaithful to one who loves you.

Applying this to our own lives, what is the greatest sin a Christian can commit? Many people feel that it is murder or lying or even coveting, but the greatest sin is unfaithfulness to God who has redeemed you and who loves you. There is no sin greater than that, my friend.

God says, "Go to your mother and contend with her. Tell her to come back to Me. Tell her to turn away from her idolatries."

> **Lest I strip her naked, and set her as in the day that she was born, and make her as a wilderness, and set her like a dry land, and slay her with thirst [Hos. 2:3].**

If she does not repent, God will judge her.

Regarding Hosea, the implication is that he was not quite as tenderhearted as the prophet Jeremiah was. I imagine he said, "I intend to have her stoned if she continues this kind of life—I have no alternative."

> **And I will not have mercy upon her children; for they be the children of whoredoms [Hos. 2:4].**

"And I will not have mercy upon her children." God is applying the sin of the nation to the individuals who compose the nation. They are illegitimate children, and God will judge them. At this time in Israel's history apparently the entire nation had turned to idolatry. God says that He will not have mercy on the children of Israel, for they are the children of harlotry.

**For their mother hath played the harlot: she that con-
ceived them hath done shamefully: for she said, I will
go after my lovers, that give me my bread and my water,
my wool and my flax, mine oil and my drink [Hos. 2:5].**

She is doing it for money! There is money in prostitution—it is one of
the big rackets in our day also. This may imply that Hosea was not a
wealthy man and was not able to provide the luxuries which Gomer
wanted; so she practiced harlotry on the side.

Israel's sin was the same: she had turned to idols, which was spiritual adultery. The people of Israel were giving the idols credit for providing for them. "I will go after my lovers, that give me my bread and
my water"—those are the necessities; "my wool and my flax, mine oil
and my drink"—those are the luxuries. And all the while it was her
loving God who was providing all these things for her.

Oh, the ingratitude of the human race—and especially professing
Christians—for all that God has provided! I hear a great deal of complaining about rising prices today. If you are one of those who are
complaining, let me ask you something: You had at least one good
meal today, didn't you? You have clothing in your closet, haven't you?
Perhaps you even have some luxuries. Who do you think provided
these? "Well," you may say, "I am an intelligent, hard-working person; I provided them for myself." I have news for you: God has provided all of those material things for you. He is the one who gave you
intelligence. He is the one who gave you a measure of health and
strength, and He is the one who provided the job for you. In fact, He is
the one who created this earth with a well-stocked pantry and with
clean air and clean water and sunshine. And yet you are ungrateful.
You can't sin much worse than that, my friend. It is true that we live in
a day when terrible crimes are being committed—stealing, lying,
murdering—but the worst sins are being committed by the children of
God who are ungrateful. I realize this is not a popular thing to say, but
here in the Book of Hosea, this is His charge against Israel.

**Therefore, behold, I will hedge up thy way with thorns,
and make a wall, that she shall not find her paths [Hos.
2:6].**

And it is my opinion that it was God who sent the Depression to my country, then the "dust bowl." I think He was speaking to us in judgment. If we had repented and had heard God at that time, we would never have had to fight World War II. We would not have been involved in warfare in Korea and then in Vietnam. If we had been sending our boys over there as missionaries to give those people the gospel, we would not have had to send our boys over there to die or to suffer in the prison camps. Back of all our problems is the big problem that we are not recognizing God.

> **And she shall follow after her lovers, but she shall not overtake them; and she shall seek them, but shall not find them: then shall she say, I will go and return to my first husband; for then was it better with me than now [Hos. 2:7].**

There comes a day when that girl who has become a harlot is no longer beautiful and her lovers lose interest in her. She finds herself being put out. This was exactly what was happening to the nation Israel. The people were saying, "Now we will go back to God."

> **For she did not know that I gave her corn, and wine, and oil, and multiplied her silver and gold, which they prepared for Baal.**

> **Therefore will I return, and take away my corn in the time thereof, and my wine in the season thereof, and will recover my wool and my flax given to cover her nakedness [Hos. 2:8–9].**

God says that He will judge Israel. I think we can apply the same thing to our own nation. We entered into difficult times beginning in World War I because we thought we were such a sophisticated nation. We have become so sophisticated that we think homosexuality should be considered normal in our society. We don't like to punish murderers anymore; we would rather accept them into our society. God calls murder and homosexuality *sin*, and He says that when these things become prevalent in a nation it is a sign that the nation is going down the tube. We have too many judges who know a great deal about the law but know nothing about how God overrules even the laws of a nation, especially when the laws are wrong and the wrong men sit on the benches of our judicial system.

> **And now will I discover her lewdness in the sight of her lovers, and none shall deliver her out of mine hand.**
>
> **I will also cause all her mirth to cease, her feast days, her new moons, and her sabbaths, and all her solemn feasts.**
>
> **And I will destroy her vines and her fig trees, whereof she hath said, These are my rewards that my lovers have given me: and I will make them a forest, and the beasts of the field shall eat them.**
>
> **And I will visit upon her the days of Baalim, wherein she burned incense to them, and she decked herself with her earrings and her jewels, and she went after her lovers, and forgat me, saith the Lord [Hos. 2:10–13].**

The greatest sin in all the world is to forget God.

> **Therefore, behold, I will allure her, and bring her into the wilderness, and speak comfortably unto her.**
>
> **And I will give her her vineyards from thence, and the valley of Achor for a door of hope: and she shall sing there, as in the days of her youth, and as in the day when she came up out of the land of Egypt [Hos. 2:14–15].**

The *valley of Achor* literally means "the valley of trouble." It refers to the incident recorded in Joshua 7. You will recall that when the children of Israel entered the Promised Land, they faced three major enemies in the center of that land who had to be conquered first so that Joshua could divide the enemy and then concentrate on taking one section at a time. The first enemy was Jericho; Jericho represents the world, and God got the victory for them at Jericho. Next they made an attack upon Ai, and they thought it would be an easy victory because Ai was a small city. Ai represents the flesh, and a great many people think they can live the Christian life in their own strength; that is, by means of the flesh—which always means defeat. Joshua was defeated at Ai, but a great lesson was learned there. God had instructed the men not to take any of the unclean things at the destruction of Jericho, but one man disobeyed. As a result, the army suffered a great defeat at Ai.

Joshua went down upon his face and cried out to God. He was as pious as I have been at times, complaining to the Lord. The Lord said to him, "Get up off your face. Israel has *sinned*. You must deal with the sin before you can have a victory." So they had to ferret out the one who had sinned and finally found him to be Achan. Achan and his property were taken to the Valley of Achor where they were destroyed and buried. From then on it was victory for Israel under General Joshua. And, friend, when you and I deal with the sins of the flesh, we will have victory in the Christian life.

"And the valley of Achor for a door of hope." In effect, God is saying, "I'll judge your sin, and after I have judged your sin, there will be a glorious, wonderful hope for you in the future."

"And she shall sing there, as in the days of her youth, and as in the day when she came up out of the land of Egypt." My friend, even today in the land of Israel, you don't find it quite like this. Although Israel is back in her land, this particular area is up near Shechem—near the place where Joseph is buried—an area characterized by Arab/Israeli conflict and not by singing. The fulfillment of this promise is still future. The day is going to come when God will bless them there.

And it shall be at that day, saith the LORD, that thou shalt call me Ishi; and shalt call me no more Baali [Hos. 2:16].

This is interesting, and the meaning of it is quite lovely. *Ishi* means "my husband," and *Baali* is connected with Baal and means "my lord or my master." You see, the people of Israel were placing the true God on the level of Baal and were trying to worship both. Of course, it is impossible to do that, and God says to them that the day is coming when Israel will call Him, "my husband."

Now let's think about this for a moment. The husband relationship implies that which is intimate and personal and is based on love. It is the highest relationship in the human family. The loveliest expression of it is found in the Song of Solomon where the bride says, "I am my beloved's, and my beloved is mine . . ." (Song 6:3).

When you have that relationship in a marriage, you have a happy home. You won't have to attend seminars that instruct you on how to live as man and wife. The secret is love; when you don't have that, you don't have anything. But if you have love, you have everything. You can work out your financial problems; you can adjust your personality conflicts; you can work together in dealing with your children if you love each other. However, if you don't love each other, you can't work out anything.

My friend, it is wonderful to have that kind of relationship with God. We can go to the Lord Jesus and say, "I love You. I belong to You." When that kind of relationship exists, Paul says, ". . . For all things are yours; whether Paul, or Apollos, or Cephas, or the world, or life, or death, or things present, or things to come; all are yours; and ye are Christ's; and Christ is God's" (1 Cor. 3:21–23). Can you call Christ yours? Do you belong to Him, and does He belong to you? If He does, then you have something good going. There is no relationship equal to that. And one day Israel will say to God, "You are my husband."

"And shalt call me no more Baali." As we have seen, Baali is connected with the hideous idol Baal, and means "my lord"—that is all it means. Remember that the Lord Jesus said, "Not every one that saith unto me, Lord, Lord, shall enter into the kingdom of heaven; but he that doeth the will of my Father which is in heaven. Many will say to me in that day, Lord, Lord, have we not prophesied in thy name? and in thy name have cast out devils? and in thy name done many wonderful works? And then will I profess unto them, I never knew you: depart from me, ye that work iniquity" (Matt. 7:21–23). Oh, my friend, the all-important thing is a personal relationship with the Lord Jesus Christ—it is not to mouth platitudes about His being your Lord and claim to be doing great things for Him. It narrows down to the thing He said to Simon Peter by the Sea of Galilee, "Lovest thou me?" Do you *love* Him?

> **For I will take away the names of Baalim out of her mouth, and they shall no more be remembered by their name [Hos. 2:17].**

Even the name of Baal will be forgotten. They will turn from idolatry.

> **And in that day will I make a covenant for them with the beasts of the field, and with the fowls of heaven, and with the creeping things of the ground: and I will break the bow and the sword and the battle out of the earth, and will make them to lie down safely [Hos. 2:18].**

In that land, as in our own land, there is a danger of many species of animals becoming extinct—some already have. God created the animals and placed them here. They have a right to this world, and in that future day He will make a covenant with them. In that day, which we designate as the Millennium, the lion and the lamb will lie down together. In our day when they lie down together, the lamb is always inside the lion, but in the Millennium they will lie down together in peace. As I am writing, there is a new interest in ecology and in the preservation of animal life. Have you ever noticed that all through the Bible God has considered the animals? Also He has considered the land itself and speaks of blessing the land. It is man who is the polluter. Man is a sinner on the inside, and he is also a sinner on the outside. He contaminates everything he touches. I recall a drive home from the Mojave Desert when the rays of the setting sun were hitting the road at an angle, and lining both sides of the road were beams and flashes of light. I have never seen anything like it. Do you know what it was? It was the broken beer bottles and whiskey bottles and perhaps a few soft drink bottles reflecting those rays of the sun! Man is a polluter everywhere he goes. Well, God says that He is going to take care of this earth. I thank God for that, because I don't think man will be able to do it.

> **And I will betroth thee unto me for ever; yea, I will betroth thee unto me in righteousness, and in judgment, and in lovingkindness, and in mercies.**

> **I will even betroth thee unto me in faithfulness: and thou shalt know the LORD [Hos. 2:19–20].**

We are seeing something very wonderful here. The word *betrothed* means literally to "woo a virgin"; it means to court a girl. If you are a married man, you can remember when your wife was a girl, and how pretty she was and how you courted her. You said a lot of sweet things then. One evening some time ago my wife and I were sitting out on the patio. I was recuperating from surgery, and we were just talking about the fact that we are getting old. I took a look at her, and I would have to say that she is getting old like I am, but I can remember that girl I first saw down in Texas with her hair as black as a raven's wing and those flashing brown eyes. She had a sultry look, let me tell you, because her complexion is dark. As we remembered those wonderful days, we got just a little sentimental. We talked about the times when we used to drive up to Fort Worth to eat in a restaurant there. We ordered steaks, and do you know what we paid for a steak in that day? It was fifty cents apiece! She was a school teacher, and I was a poor preacher; so I made her pay for her own—even at fifty cents! I've tried to make up for that through the years since then, I can assure you. To woo a virgin is a wonderful experience. That is what God said He would do to Israel. What a beautiful, lovely picture this is. God says, "I intend to win you for Myself."

How is God going to do this? He says, "I will betroth thee unto me in righteousness, and in judgment, and in lovingkindness, and in mercies." You see, there was mercy under the Mosaic system, too. You will find that there was love in law just as there is law in love. You cannot completely segregate one from the other.

This is another reason why I do not think the present return of Israel to their land is a fulfillment of prophecy. It certainly does not fulfill this one. God says that when He woos Israel and brings her back into the land it will be in righteousness and in justice and in loving-kindness and in mercies. Today Israel is just like any other nation. Some think they are unnecessarily brutal, but they are on the defensive and their survival depends on a strong defense system. They are not back in the land of Israel in fulfillment of prophecy. Although they have returned to the land, they have not returned to the Lord. When they do return to the Lord, there will be blessing.

"I will even betroth thee unto me in faithfulness." They never were faithful in the past. In fact, they are very much like the apostate church in our day.

"And thou shalt know the Lord." They certainly do not know Him today.

> **And it shall come to pass in that day, I will hear, saith the Lord, I will hear the heavens, and they shall hear the earth [Hos. 2:21].**

"In that day" is a technical expression which refers to the last days as they pertain to the nation Israel, the Great Tribulation period, and the coming of Christ to set up His Kingdom on earth.

"I will hear the heavens, and they shall hear the earth"—heaven and earth will be in tune.

> **And the earth shall hear the corn, and the wine, and the oil; and they shall hear Jezreel [Hos. 2:22].**

"Jezreel" means that God will scatter or sow them, but in that future day God will regather them.

And I will sow her unto me in the earth; and I will have mercy upon her that had not obtained mercy; and I will say to them which were not my people, Thou art my people; and they shall say, Thou art my God [Hos. 2:23].

These final two verses are a play upon the names of Gomer's children. Not only will God regather them, but they will no longer be Lo-ruhamah, like the unpitied daughter of harlotry. God will have mercy upon them. In our day Israel is Lo-ammi—"not my people," but in that future day God will say, "You are My people," and they will say, "You are my God." My friend, they are not saying that today; they are not turning to God. This is a prophecy for the Millennium.

CHAPTER 3

THEME: Hosea commanded to take Gomer again

Although Hosea finds out that his wife has proved unfaithful, he is commanded to go and take Gomer again.

> **Then said the LORD unto me, Go yet, love a woman beloved of her friend, yet an adulteress, according to the love of the LORD toward the children of Israel, who look to other gods, and love flagons of wine [Hos. 3:1].**

"Go yet, love a woman"—that is, love your wife; she is your woman. "Beloved of her friend"—Hosea loved her although she had been unfaithful.

"Yet an adulteress, according to the love of the LORD toward the children of Israel who look to other gods, and love flagons of wine." "Flagons of wine" should actually be translated as "cakes of raisins." This is a reference to the cakes of raisins which were used in the sacrificial feasts of the Canaanites. They were a part of the heathen worship of idols, which the children of Israel had adopted. You see that God is making an application here. In effect He says to Hosea, "Now you know how I feel. I want you to go and take Gomer again. She's been unfaithful to you, but you are to love her and take her back. That is what I am going to do with My people. Israel has been unfaithful to Me, and I am going to punish her, but some day I will bring her back to Myself."

> **So I bought her to me for fifteen pieces of silver, and for an homer of barley, and an half homer of barley [Hos. 3:2].**

Perhaps Gomer had sold herself to some group of racketeers who were running brothels in that land. Hosea had to go buy her back. "So I bought her to me."

Do you know that you and I have been redeemed? The picture here is not very pretty—that is the reason it is not being preached more today. We hear a great deal in conservative circles about dedication, about commitment, and about turning your life over to the Lord. But, my friend, the first thing you need to do is to come as a sinner to God—He has to redeem you. Just as Hosea bought this harlot, that is the way God redeemed us. Until you and I see that, we can know nothing of real commitment to God.

"So I bought her to me for fifteen pieces of silver, and for an homer of barley, and an half homer of barley." Gomer wasn't worth it, and we are not worth the redemption price which was paid for us. "Forasmuch as ye know that ye were not redeemed with corruptible things, as silver and gold . . . but with the precious blood of Christ . . ." (1 Pet. 1:18–19). He had to shed His blood; He had to suffer and die that you and I might be redeemed. Why? Because we were lost sinners, sold under sin.

I have a friend who is a great preacher, but he has gotten to the place where he no longer mentions the gospel. He does not mention the fact that a man must come to God as a sinner. Oh, he tells people, "You ought to love Jesus. You ought to serve God and obey Him," and all that sort of thing. But, my friend, that is not where you begin. You might as well go out to a graveyard and say, "Listen, fellas and girls, let's all start doing better. Let's all start committing our lives to the Lord." Why, everybody out there is dead! They can't do anything. And until we have come to God for salvation, you and I are dead in trespasses and sins. We have no life to commit to Him. Until the sin issue is settled—until we are born again and have received a new nature—we can do nothing that is pleasing to God.

And I said unto her, Thou shalt abide for me many days; thou shalt not play the harlot, and thou shalt not be for another man: so will I also be for thee [Hos. 3:3].

A man told me the sad story not long ago of how he had found out that his wife was unfaithful to him. He had actually had her followed by a detective to establish the facts. Imagine the feeling of that man! Oh, what a heartbreak it was to find out that she was unfaithful to him. I cannot think of anything worse than that. And God says to His people, "That is what you have been doing. You've been playing the harlot. Oh, you call Me, 'Lord,' but you have gone after other gods, you have turned from Me and no longer serve Me."

The Lord Jesus also said in Matthew 7:22–23, "Many will say to me in that day, Lord, Lord, have we not prophesied in thy name? and in thy name have cast out devils? and in thy name done many wonderful works? And then will I profess unto them, I never knew you. . . ." Now I am going to say perhaps the strongest thing you have ever heard: If a so-called church has a man in the pulpit who denies the Word of God, denies the deity of Christ, and denies that He died for sinners, it is not a church. It is a brothel—a spiritual *brothel!* I didn't say that; God says that right here. This is the strongest language you can imagine, and you can understand why Hosea was not elected "Man of the Year" in Israel at that particular time. He didn't win any popularity contest in his hometown, you can be sure. He is telling his people, "You have become a *brothel* as a nation. You've turned to idolatry and have turned from the living and true God."

Verses 4 and 5 of this chapter are probably two of the most important prophetic verses which supply an answer to those students of prophecy who have begun to set dates for the coming of the Lord. Although this is a brief chapter, having only five verses, it is one of the great prophetic passages in the Word of God. Dr. Charles Feinberg, a Jewish believer and an outstanding Hebrew scholar, says of this chapter, "It rightfully takes its place among the greatest prophetic pronouncements in the whole revelation of God."

In connection with this passage, you ought to read chapters 9—11 of the Epistle to the Romans. I consider those chapters to be the dispensational section of the epistle which concerns the nation Israel. In chapter 9 you have the past dealings of God with Israel, in chapter 10 His present dealings with Israel, and in chapter 11 His future dealings with them.

Now concerning Israel, Hosea writes—

**For the children of Israel shall abide many days without
a king, and without a prince, and without a sacrifice,
and without an image, and without an ephod, and without teraphim [Hos. 3:4].**

"For the children of Israel shall abide *many days* without a king." You
will notice that He does not give a specific number of days. This is
unusual because the children of Israel were told three times that they
were to be put out of their land and they would be returned three
times. Each time God put them out of that land, He told them how
long they would be out—except the last time. The first time, God told
Abraham, "I am going to give you this land—it's yours, but I am going
to put your children out of this land for 430 years. They will be down
in the land of Egypt, and after 430 years, I will bring them back." They
did come back—that prophecy was literally fulfilled. A second time,
God said through Jeremiah, "Because of your sins, you are going to be
down there for seventy years." Again, that was fulfilled literally. Now,
here Hosea is speaking to the northern kingdom (which never actually
returned to the land), and he says, "Israel shall abide many days without a king."

How long is "many days"? Right now we have some folk who are
saying that the Lord Jesus is going to come again by A.D. 2000. I do not
know where they find that in Scripture! They sound as if they have a
private line into heaven! And at least one other to whom I have listened says that the generation living today is the one that is going to
see the coming of Christ. May I say, that sounds good to a lot of un-
taught Christians, but you cannot find such teaching in the Word of
God. Nowhere does Scripture tell us how long the time will be until
His return. We have a lot of sensational prophecy-mongers about today.

Why did the Lord say "many days" and not give us the specific
number? It is because in the interval between the time Israel left the
land in A.D. 70 and the time at which they will return, He has been
calling out a people to His name from among the Gentiles and has
been building His church. I want to say first of all that I believe we are
living in the last days. Someone will say, "Do you mean then that the

Lord will be coming soon?" Well, I do not know how soon because we have been in the "last days" for more than nineteen hundred years. The Lord Jesus said, "Behold, I come quickly . . ." (Rev. 3:11; 22:7), and that was nineteen hundred years ago. Therefore I am not prepared to say He will come tomorrow or next week or next year or even in this century. I just don't happen to know that. But I do believe we are seeing the setting of the stage, and the action will begin when the church is removed from this earth.

The reason the date is not given here in Hosea is that in Scripture the church is nameless and dateless. We who belong to the true church are a heavenly people, having no name. I suppose some of you folk thought the name of the church was Baptist or Presbyterian or Methodist or Christian or even Independent. I have news for you: the church has no name; Scripture has never given it a name. The Greek word *ecclesia* simply means "a called-out body." He is calling out a body today which is going to be His bride. I could make a suggestion today for a name for the church. In the parable of the pearl of great price (see Matt. 13:45–46), the pearl represents the church which the merchantman, Jesus, came and bought. He paid a big price for the church, you know. The word for pearl is *margarites*. If the church is to have any name at all, I think it should be Margaret. Have you ever heard of the Margaret Church? One time I told a fellow that I went to the Margaret Church; he thought I was kidding, but I really was serious about it.

The church is nameless, and it is also dateless. If you had met Simon Peter an hour before the Holy Spirit came on the Day of Pentecost and you had asked him, "Do you know what's going to happen here in a little while?" he would have said, "No. What's going to happen?" He didn't know, because the birth of the church had been announced, but no date had been given. And we are not given the date of the Rapture, the time when the church will be removed from this earth. For that reason we are told "the children of Israel shall abide *many days* without a king"—no specific time period is given to us.

Israel is going to abide many days "without a king." There are those in that land today who claim that they can tell you the tribe to which they belong. I have serious doubts about that, but they make that claim. However, there is no Israelite living today who can say, "I am in the line of David, and I have a right to the throne of David." The only One who can claim that is this moment sitting at God's right hand. He is the Lord Jesus, King of kings and Lord of lords. Israel has rejected their King.

"Without a prince"—they have no one to succeed to the throne. If the Lord Jesus Christ is not their Messiah, they have none and have no prospect of one.

"Without a sacrifice." Luke 21:24 tells us that ". . . Jerusalem shall be trodden down of the Gentiles, until the times of the Gentiles be fulfilled." Therefore, many people argue that we must be to the end of the "times of the Gentiles" because Israel now has Jerusalem. Do they really have Jerusalem today? All of the holy places in old Jerusalem are in the hands of either the Moslems, the Russian Catholics, the Greek Catholics, the Armenian Church, or the Roman Catholics. And all of them have built cathedrals or churches over these spots. Israel does not possess these sacred spots, and they dare not touch them. I said once to a Jewish guide with whom I had become acquainted, "You have Jerusalem now. Why don't you go and tear down that Mosque of Omar and put up your own temple?" He said, "What do you want us to do—start World War III?" That would surely start it, my friend—you can be sure of that. Israel does not possess that temple area, and they do not have a sacrifice today. The only holy place they have is the Wailing Wall—they are still at the Wailing Wall. They have no sacrifice except the one which you and I have—Jesus. He died nineteen hundred years ago outside the city, was raised from the dead, and is today at God's right hand.

"Without an image." God did not give Israel any images. He had said to them, "Thou shalt not make unto thee any graven image, or any likeness of any thing . . ." (Exod. 20:4). But He had given them many things; for instance, "an ephod" and "a teraphim." The ephod was the sacred garment worn by the high priest. Teraphim were small objects which they carried around like good luck charms and which they began to worship. God says here that they are going to get away from idolatry, that they will not have any images. That is one thing that you can say about Israel today—they are not in idolatry. Although they have not turned to God, they certainly have turned away from idolatry.

Afterward shall the children of Israel return, and seek the LORD their God, and David their king; and shall fear the LORD and his goodness in the latter days [Hos. 3:5].

"Afterward shall the children of Israel return." *Afterward* does not mean in the year A.D. 2000. I do not know when it will be, but they are going to return to the land according to God's timetable.

When they do return, this is the way they will return: they shall "seek the LORD their God, and David their king; and shall fear the LORD and his goodness in the latter days." I am going to say something that may be very startling to you. They have returned to that land, and it is remarkable what has happened over there, but it is not the fulfillment of this prophecy. The prophecy says that when they return, they will return to God, and there is no real turning to God in that land. It is the belief of at least two outstanding prophetic students whom I know, that Israel may be put out of that land again before we have the real fulfillment of this prophecy. When they return to the land, they will also return to God.

There is much evidence that Israel has not turned to the Lord. When they celebrated their twentieth anniversary as a nation some years ago, they displayed a large motto which read, "Science will bring peace to this land." The Scriptures say it is the Messiah who is going to bring peace. They are not turning to the Messiah but to science. They are looking to prosperity and depending upon economics. Sometime ago they had a large economic conference which was attended by one of the Rockefellers and one of the Fords. There were a hundred outstanding men there who each put up a million dollars to invest in that land. They are building over there like I have never seen anywhere else.

A very reputable missionary in Israel was specifically asked this question: "How many true Christians are there in this land today?" This missionary is an intelligent man who speaks several languages. He was a professor who became a Christian and is doing missionary work there. He gave this reply: "Today in Israel there are fewer than three hundred Israelites who are real believers in Christ." I know that that statement may cause a great deal of discussion and disagreement because there are those who are saying that hundreds are turning to Christ in that land. That just does not happen to be true. There are actually more Arab Christians in Israel than Jewish Christians. Missionary work in Israel is really a tough job, and there are very few missionaries in that land. Israel has not returned to God.

I know when I insist that this present return to the land is not the fulfillment of the Word of God, it is contrary to what you hear so often today. However, this prophecy is evidence of that fact; and, when we consider the whole of the Word of God and not just a verse here and there, we must face up to the fact that this return is not a fulfillment of prophecy.

Many ridiculous things result when people take a verse here or there and say that what is happening in Israel is a fulfillment of prophecy. We heard some time ago that they were shipping Indiana stone over to Israel to build the temple. If you have been to Jerusalem, you know that one thing they do *not* need is stone! Jerusalem is located on a rocky place and every hill around it, including the Mount of Olives, is loaded with rocks. Now, if Indiana wants to buy some stone, I could tell them where to get it: Israel would be glad to export some of her stone.

Another example of so-called fulfilled prophecy is the argument that the growing of oranges in Israel is a fulfillment of the "strange slips" which Isaiah said would grow in that land (see Isa. 17:10). However, in the Song of Solomon where it speaks of the apples and the apple tree, that is actually the orange tree. Oranges grow in that land, and it is the belief of some that oranges were taken from there to Spain and then to Florida and California. Israel is the land that grows oranges, and they are not a "strange slip." How ridiculous these things can become! We need to stay close to the Word of God and not become one of these prophetic fanatics who are abroad today.

"And shall fear the Lord and his goodness in the latter days." "The latter days" are yet in the future. They refer to the nation Israel and to the time beginning with the Great Tribulation and going through the second coming of Christ and on into the Millennium.

CHAPTER 4

THEME: Israel guilty before God

From this point on in the Book of Hosea we will not be seeing much about the private and personal life of the prophet. Beginning actually with the two closing verses of the previous chapter, the private life of Hosea fades into the background, and the emphasis is now upon the Lord and the faithless nation of Israel which has been playing the harlot. We have left that section of the book which is personal, and in chapters 4—14 we will be dealing with that which is *prophetic.*

ISRAEL GUILTY BEFORE GOD

Out of the heartbreaking experience in his own home, Hosea now comes to speak to the nation—and he knows how God feels about them. Everything that has been said up to this point has been in the way of generalization. God has said, "They have sinned. They have played the harlot and been unfaithful to Me." Now God is going to bring them into court, spell out certain charges against them, and prove those charges. The message of chapter 4 is that Israel is guilty of lawlessness, immorality, ignorance of God's Word, and idolatry. We can compare this chapter with the first chapter of Isaiah in which Isaiah speaks to the southern kingdom, spelling out God's charge against that nation.

I believe that you could interchange these same sins of Israel with the sins of our own nation. It is true that the nation Israel was God's chosen people, and He gave the Mosaic Law to them. However, we need to understand this: the Law is His pattern for any nation which wants to be blessed. Therefore, I think that our nation is guilty of the same sins that Israel was guilty of when God judged them and sent them into captivity. Someone will disagree with me and say, "Well, we're not idolaters." My friend, covetousness is idolatry, and I do not know of a nation that is more greedy and worships the almighty dollar more than this nation of ours today. We might read the Book of Hosea and point our finger at Israel and say, "It is a shame how they turned from God," but we need to look around and see if the same thing is not true of us.

In the first verse of this chapter, the Lord confronts Israel with the fact that they have no knowledge of Him—

Hear the word of the LORD, ye children of Israel: for the LORD hath a controversy with the inhabitants of the land, because there is no truth, nor mercy, nor knowledge of God in the land [Hos. 4:1].

He says three things here: there is no mercy; there is no truth; and there is no knowledge of God in the land. These people had become brainwashed through their idolatry. Although God had instructed them to be merciful, they were no longer showing mercy. The Lord had told them in Leviticus 19:10, "And thou shalt not glean thy vineyard, neither shalt thou gather every grape of thy vineyard; thou shalt leave them for the poor and stranger: I am the LORD your God." In other words, He said, "This is the way I take care of the poor, and you are to do this also." Why? "Because I am the Lord your God, and I am a holy God." The people had forgotten this—there was no knowledge of God in the land—and they were no longer being merciful. Oh, there was a great deal of religion, but no real knowledge of God.

Notice that they were breaking the Ten Commandments:

By swearing, and lying, and killing, and stealing, and committing adultery, they break out, and blood toucheth blood [Hos. 4:2].

In each of these sins they were breaking the Ten Commandments. Read them in the twentieth chapter of Exodus: "Thou shalt not kill. Thou shalt not commit adultery. Thou shalt not steal. Thou shalt not bear false witness . . ." (Exod. 20:13–16). And all of this that they were doing was happening even among relatives—"blood toucheth blood."

I want to say something very carefully, and I want you to follow me very carefully. God gave the Ten Commandments, which were only a part of the Mosaic system, to the nation Israel, but in them God expressed His will.

The church today is not under the Ten Commandments as the way of salvation or the way to live the Christian life, but that does not mean that we can break the commandments; it simply means that He has called us to a higher plane of living and has enabled us so to live by the power of the Holy Spirit.

However, since through the Ten Commandments God expresses His will, they are a pattern for the laws of every nation. The nation Israel, which He chose and dealt with, furnishes a pattern to the other nations of the world. We have a so-called Christian civilization in Europe today. It has never really been Christian but has had the semblance of Christianity because its laws were patterned after the Ten Commandments. These laws are the laws for all nations.

God has said, "Thou shalt not kill. Thou shalt not commit adultery," and there are other things which He has condemned in Scripture. God has condemned drunkenness, and He has condemned homosexuality. He uses the strongest language in speaking of homosexuality. God says that when a people or an individual indulges in that, He will give them up. God gave Israel up to captivity because they were guilty of indulging in these sins.

We in the United States today are guilty of the same thing: there is no knowledge of God in this land. Oh, I know that there seems to be a church on every corner and on Sunday mornings you can hear church bells everywhere, but a very small percentage of the population actually attends church, and very few are really being reached with the Word of God. There is a Gideon Bible in every hotel or motel room in which I stay, but I do not know how much they are being read. The Gideons report that they receive many letters telling of conversions—and I thank God for that—but I am afraid that many of the Bibles are never opened. My point is that, although we have the Bible freely available, we are actually a nation of Bible ignoramuses. We do not know the Word of God today in this land. For example, a political leader some time ago made the statement on television that the four Gospels contradict one another; he not only misquoted Scripture, he also misinterpreted it. I would have liked to demand equal time to answer him that there is no contradiction in the four Gospels. When a man makes a statement like that, he reveals a woeful ignorance of the Word of God.

The consumption of alcohol is another area in which our land is in the same condition as Israel was in that day. We were told a few years ago that there were 128 cocktail parties every day in Washington, D.C. With the trend as it is, I am sure that number has increased greatly. Whatever the actual statistics, we know that there is a great deal of drinking going on in our nation's capital. Like Israel, we too are being brainwashed by liberal propaganda. A local newspaper in one large city in Southern California dared to publish an article a number of years ago with the following headline: "Alcoholics Cost Area Businesses Ten Million Dollars." People cry out about the high cost of living, the high cost of war, and the high cost of government—all of which is true—but who is crying out against liquor today? We are told that millions of American workers are alcoholics. What do you suppose that has to do with the cost of what we buy at the store today? Someone may say, "Preacher, this is none of your business." My friend, the pulpit has become extremely silent on these issues, but I must insist that our government and our nation are engaged in gross immorality and are breaking the Ten Commandments. And we will not get by with it as a nation. An alarming percentage of the deaths on U.S. highways and streets is the result of alcohol drinking. We have had much protest about the killing in war, but I have found no one leading a protest in front of a brewery or a cocktail lounge.

It is argued in our day that alcoholism is a disease and not a sin. That has been answered by a medical doctor, who writes:

Alcoholism, a disease? If so:

It is the only disease contracted by an act of will.

It is the only disease that is habit forming.

It is the only disease that comes in a bottle.

It is the only disease causing hundreds of thousands of family disruptions.

It is the only disease promoting crime and brutality.

It is the only disease contributing to hundreds of thousands of automobile accidents.

It is the only disease playing a major part in over 50 percent of the more than 50,000 annual highway deaths.

It is the only disease which is sold by license.

It is the only disease that is bought in grocery stores, drug stores, and well-marked retail outlets.

It is the only disease that is taxed by the government. . . .

Our eyes have been shut to all these facts because the liquor interests have tremendous control in our country, and we have been brainwashed by them. As a result, our nation sinks lower and lower.

We have what we call the "new morality" today, but it isn't new at all. Israel was practicing it way back yonder in 700 B.C. They were breaking all the commandments, and God condemned them for it. It wasn't even the "new" morality in their day, for homosexuality was practiced as far back as the day of Sodom and Gomorrah, cities which were judged by God and destroyed because of it. Today we have legislatures which are filled with men who are ignorant of the Word of God and ignorant of the commandments which have been basic for this nation, and they are passing legislation which condones the life style of sexual perverts.

The liberal church argues that homosexuals are not sinners, but may I say to you, Jesus Christ says to homosexuals, "Ye must be born again" (see John 3:7). He can deliver you from it. When homosexuality is treated for what it really is—sin—then God can deal with it.

We as a nation are doomed as much as Israel was condemned and sent into captivity. After all, they were God's chosen people and we are not—by no stretch of the imagination can we make that claim. However, we have here in Hosea the basis on which God judges nations, and the United States stands condemned as did Israel. The pulpits in this country are strangely silent in this connection, and one reason for that is that they seldom if ever study the Book of Hosea; he is one of the forgotten prophets.

Therefore shall the land mourn, and every one that dwelleth therein shall languish, with the beasts of the field, and with the fowls of heaven; yea, the fishes of the sea also shall be taken away [Hos. 4:3].

"Therefore shall the land mourn." Suddenly we have found in this country that we are polluting everything around us. But when I was a boy in southern Oklahoma, we used to go swimming in old Phillips Creek, and the water was so clear you could see twenty-five feet to the bottom of that creek. Today it smells to high heaven. We've polluted the land, and the land is mourning today.

Another interesting thing is that a few years ago there was plenty of everything—the granaries were filled with grain—but today we often hear about the scarcity of this or that. You see, when God judges a nation, the land itself is involved and even the beasts and fowls suffer because of the sin of man.

Yet let no man strive, nor reprove another: for thy people are as they that strive with the priest [Hos. 4:4].

The priest in that day was not doing his duty; he was not warning the people. Therefore, God raised up the prophets.

Therefore shalt thou fall in the day, and the prophet also shall fall with thee in the night, and I will destroy thy mother [Hos. 4:5].

"And I will destroy thy mother"—that is, God will destroy the nation. There were false prophets in Israel—even as we have false prophets today—telling the people, "Everything is going to be all right. We live in a new age. The Bible is an outmoded book, and the Ten Commandments belong to our grandfathers and grandmothers. We have learned to be broad-minded and tolerant." My friend, the truth is that we are a dirty lot, and we have sunk very low as a nation and as a people.

Verse 6 is perhaps the most familiar verse in the Book of Hosea—

My people are destroyed for lack of knowledge: because thou hast rejected knowledge, I will also reject thee, that thou shalt be no priest to me: seeing thou hast forgotten the law of thy God, I will also forget thy children [Hos. 4:6].

"My people are destroyed for lack of knowledge." The background of their sin was a lack of knowledge of the Word of God. My friend, if you are a Christian, the minute you get away from the Word of God, you are doomed to failure in the Christian life. Regardless of the number of conferences or seminars you attend that tell you how to be a success in your home, in your business, and in your social life, you will be a failure. This book makes it crystal-clear that we do not live the Christian life by these little gimmicks and methods, but by a personal knowledge of the Word of God. This is the reason I am concerned with teaching the Word of God—and the reason I teach even the Book of Hosea. People are destroyed for lack of knowledge.

"Because thou hast rejected knowledge, I will also reject thee, that thou shalt be no priest to me." God intended that the whole nation of Israel be priests unto Him; in the Millennium they will be that. But at this time, God says, "You are not even going to *have* priests."

"Seeing thou hast forgotten the law of thy God, I will also forget thy children." God says to the people of this nation, "I will forget you, because you have forgotten Me." Because they have gone through a long, sordid history of departing from the Lord, they have now come to the time of judgment. God has proved His case against these people; in the beginning of the chapter He enumerated their sins—they have broken the Ten Commandments. Therefore He hands down His decision that He is going to judge them.

As they were increased, so they sinned against me: therefore will I change their glory into shame [Hos. 4:7].

God had promised Abraham to bless the nation by multiplying them, and the nation did increase, but all that it did was bring more sinners into the world. After all, that is what happened when I was born—another sinner came into the world. But, thank God, the grace of God reached down, and someone gave me the Word of God, and I was able to trust Christ as my Savior. However, these people were ignorant and had no knowledge of the Word of God.

"Therefore will I change their glory into shame." Now the "glory" of Israel was the temple with the Shekinah glory upon it—His visible presence with the nation and His definite leading of them, and their witness of monotheism to the world of polytheism of their day as they worshiped the living and true God. That was their glory, and it brought the Queen of Sheba from the ends of the earth.

God is saying through Hosea, "I will remove My glory from you. I'll remove My blessing from you, and I will judge you by letting the enemy come upon you and take you into captivity."

Of course the enemy is going to be able to say, "Look, they said they were God's chosen people, but look what is happening to them! Apparently their God is not a very strong God." My friend, we are seeing today in this land of ours something very similar to that. God is judging many churches, and He is closing many doors. We are inclined to say, "Isn't it a shame to see a decline in a certain church." Well, maybe *God* is closing the door. We need to recognize that God can afford to judge His own people, and this is what He is doing.

They eat up the sin of my people, and they set their heart on their iniquity [Hos. 4:8].

The people not only sinned, but they liked to brag about it. As a young fellow I ran with a pretty fast crowd from the bank where I worked. Especially on Monday mornings we liked to brag about what we had done on our weekend, and the blacker the sin was, the more we enjoyed bragging about it. That is what these people were doing—"they set their heart on their iniquity."

And there shall be, like people, like priest: and I will punish them for their ways, and reward them their doings [Hos. 4:9].

The unfortunate thing was that the priesthood in Israel had sunk down to the level of the congregation. When I started out in the ministry, I wore a Prince Albert coat and a wing collar (a friend of mine told me that I looked like a mule looking over a whitewashed fence!), but I soon gave that up and began to dress just like the man sitting out there in the pew. Although I'm no different from the man in the pew, I do want to give out the Word of God in the pulpit and not sink to the level of the man of the world when I'm out of the pulpit. There are many ministers who seek to be "good guys." One man boasting of his pastor said, "You know, my preacher comes out to our golf club and plays golf with us." That much sounds good. I think it is great to mix with folk like that. Then he added, "And after the game he goes into the barroom and has a drink with us. He is just one of the fellows. I sure do like him." Well, I wonder what God thinks of him—"Like people, like priest: and I will punish them for their ways, and reward them their doings."

> **For they shall eat, and not have enough: they shall commit whoredom, and shall not increase: because they have left off to take heed to the LORD [Hos. 4:10].**

"For they shall eat, and not have enough"—in other words, famine is coming to the land. Who would have believed that we would ever hear anything about scarcities in this country—that there would ever be times when we could not buy meat or bread in the market—yet we have learned in recent years that such circumstances are a real possibility. Again may I say that I believe God judged this nation in the years of the Depression and the "dust bowl," but no one listened to Him. Then we had to fight World War II, and still we didn't come back to God. We have had very little peace and a whole lot of troubles since then.

"They shall commit whoredom, and shall not increase." I know what I am saying when I tell you that you can never, never enjoy the sexual relationship in the way in which God really wants you to enjoy it unless it is within the bonds of marriage. When you can put your arms around a woman whom you have been loving and can say to her,

"I love you above everything else in the world," then it is wonderful and there will be an increase. Otherwise, there is really no satisfaction in it; it is just a temporary sort of release, and you hate yourself afterward. I know that some of you know that, and God knows that—He is spelling that out for us here.

Whoredom and wine and new wine take away the heart [Hos. 4:11].

Part of our problems in Washington, D.C. today are caused by these two sins—harlotry or adultery and liquor. They are responsible for men lying and doing any number of crooked things. This is not confined to just one political party or group; the whole crowd is guilty. One writer said that in Washington you do not know whom to trust— what a sad commentary on our nation! Do not tell me that the "new" morality is working today. It didn't work for Israel either when they got away from the Word of God and decided to try something new. In the northern kingdom they had sin galore. They put up two golden calves to replace God and practiced Baal worship which involved the grossest form of immorality.

My people ask counsel at their stocks, and their staff declareth unto them: for the spirit of whoredoms hath caused them to err, and they have gone a-whoring from under their God [Hos. 4:12].

He is speaking here of the harlotry, the spiritual adultery, which is turning from God—they went to inquire of idols. Today we find people running after the gurus of India. One of the gurus who came to this country said very candidly that he had come for the money and that it was nothing in the world but a religious racket as far as he was concerned—yet people went after him! People are going off into all types of things today, including the worship of Satan. I have a newspaper clipping which reports that a group of Satan cultists tortured and beat a seventeen-year-old youth to death, believing he was an undercover narcotics agent. The worship of Satan today is certainly not helping the morality of our country. And in Israel, idolatry simply led them into gross immorality and finally to God's judgment.

> **They sacrifice upon the tops of the mountains, and burn incense upon the hills, under oaks and poplars and elms, because the shadow thereof is good: therefore your daughters shall commit whoredom, and your spouses shall commit adultery [Hos. 4:13].**

They put their idols on top of a hill under a grove of trees. The center of this idolatrous worship was in these groves; it was cool there and a nice place to go.

"Therefore your daughters shall commit whoredom, and your spouses shall commit adultery." Our idolatry in this country today is covetousness and greed, and it has caused many a family to try to get on in the world. They want to move to a better neighborhood, to have a swimming pool, and to have a boat. They say they are doing it for the children—but all of a sudden the children leave the home. There are thousands and thousands of young people wandering up and down this country and all over the world. I have seen them in the Hawaiian Islands, and I talked to three of them in Constitution Square in Athens some time ago. There were two young men and a young lady, and I am sure they were not beyond their teens—one of them could have been twenty. I tried to talk with them as they sat there under the influence of drugs. They told me, "We're nobody. We don't count. We've dropped out." What has happened to them? The problem is back there in the home. Their parents are idolatrous, worshiping the almighty dollar. We have forgotten God. We've turned away from the living and true God, and we no longer worship Him. We need to turn to the Savior who can redeem us and help us.

> **I will not punish your daughters when they commit whoredom, nor your spouses when they commit adultery: for themselves are separated with whores, and they sacrifice with harlots: therefore the people that doth not understand shall fall [Hos. 4:14].**

God says that ignorance of the law excuses no one. He is saying, "Although these people have gone off into sin, I am not going to judge them for the sin they are committing right now. I am going to judge them because they have turned from the living and true God and from His way." I made this point to a man on the golf course who joined with my two preacher friends and myself to make a foursome. He said he guessed he was a sinner going to hell because of the various sins he had committed. I said to him, "You know, you're not going to hell because you commit those sins." He said, "What do you mean I'm not going to hell? I thought that's what you preachers say." I told him, "This preacher never said that. You're going to hell because you have rejected Jesus Christ." Israel was not judged because they had become harlots, but because they had turned from the living and true God.

> **Though thou, Israel, play the harlot, yet let not Judah offend; and come not ye unto Gilgal, neither go ye up to Beth-aven, nor swear, The Lord liveth [Hos. 4:15].**

God is saying, "I am going to hold Judah back. I will not judge Judah yet. And Judah, don't you come up and worship these calves which Israel has put up here."

> **For Israel slideth back as a backsliding heifer: now the Lord will feed them as a lamb in a large place [Hos. 4:16].**

I want to look at what backsliding really is. A great many people think that backsliding is when you have become a Christian, have joined the church, and then drop back into sin. That is not backsliding in the way it is used here—God illustrates it so that you cannot miss its meaning: "For Israel slideth back as a backsliding heifer." In the little town in which I lived in southern Oklahoma as a boy, there lived next door to us a rancher who had a big cattle ranch and two boys who were about my age. We three played together. We enjoyed riding heifers out in the lot. We would tie a rope around them—as we said in that day, a bellyband—and we would hold on to that until the heifer bucked us off. Every now and then that rancher would need to load up some of those heifers into his wagon to take them to market. He had a runway constructed out of boards which he would put at the back end of the wagon, and then he would try to run the heifers up that. He put a rope around the heifer to lead her up and then would have someone push her from the rear. The heifer would go up part of the way, and then she would stiffen those front feet of hers. You know what would happen? You couldn't push her, and you couldn't pull her. She would simply start sliding backwards. My friend, that's what backsliding is—"a backsliding heifer." Israel was stiffening her front feet, and instead of being led of God, she was slipping backward all the time. My friend, you are backsliding when you turn your back on God, stiffen that little neck of yours and that little mind of yours, and you say, "I don't have to obey God's Word." When you refuse to go the way God wants to lead you, then you are backsliding. God called Israel a backsliding heifer.

The word *backsliding* is used three times in this book. It is used in Scripture only by Jeremiah and Hosea, both of whom spoke to a nation ready to go into captivity. Israel and Judah were guilty of backsliding, guilty of refusing to be led of God and refusing to come to God.

Ephraim is joined to idols: let him alone [Hos. 4:17].

"Ephraim" occurs thirty-six times in this book. God has picked out the name of one of the ten tribes in the north and applied it to all ten of the tribes. I used to wonder just how God used this term: was it a term of endearment or a term of ridicule? I have come to the conclusion that it was a term of endearment, actually His pet name for the northern kingdom. These ten tribes had revolted, and Israel in the north actually had no name as a nation; it was Judah in the south who was really the nation. I think God gave this to them as a pet name—Ephraim. It is used throughout this Book of Hosea.

"Ephraim is joined to idols: let him alone." God says this in a longing sort of way but with a note of finality. If a man continues in a backslidden condition, refusing to listen to God, there will come a day when God can no longer speak to that man.

**Their drink is sour: they have committed whoredom
continually: her rulers with shame do love, Give ye
[Hos. 4:18].**

"Their drink is sour"—You will become an alcoholic if you keep
drinking, my friend. And it is not a disease; it is sin.

"They have committed whoredom continually: her rulers with
shame do love." The sad thing is that men high in our government,
instead of using language that is clean and chaste, love to curse and to
drink. They love shame more than glory.

**The wind hath bound her up in her wings, and they
shall be ashamed because of their sacrifices [Hos. 4:19].**

People are carried away by every wind of doctrine, and God says that
they are going to be made ashamed before it is over.

CHAPTER 5

THEME: Israel turns from God and God turns from Israel

This chapter continues to deal with the sin of the northern kingdom and the fact that judgment is coming upon them; therefore it is not a very happy or pleasant section of the Word of God.

We must keep in mind the personal background of the prophet Hosea. As a young man, he fell in love with a very lovely, beautiful young lady who became a prostitute. I imagine that she was attracted to prostitution by the money, by the fact that she would be able to get the luxuries that she otherwise could not have had. God sent Hosea to marry her in spite of this. He loved her and married her. After she had borne three children, again she played the harlot. And again Hosea went after her—he bought her and brought her back to himself. Hosea had a broken heart and a broken home. With that background, he said to the northern kingdom of Israel, "God says that you are playing the harlot, that you have been unfaithful to Him. I know exactly how He feels. He loves you and will never let you go, but He is going to judge you because of your sin."

ISRAEL TURNS FROM GOD AND
GOD TURNS FROM ISRAEL

God begins by condemning the leadership in the nation—the priests and the king.

> Hear ye this, O priests; and hearken, ye house of Israel; and give ye ear, O house of the king; for judgment is toward you, because ye have been a snare on Mizpah, and a net spread upon Tabor [Hos. 5:1].

"Mizpah" was in the southwest section of the kingdom, and "Tabor" is Mount Tabor which was way up in the northeast section of the kingdom. In other words, the people were worshiping idols under every green tree they could find—there were idols all over the land.

He speaks to the priests and to the king as representing the leadership of the nation. We saw in chapter 4 that God said, "Like people, like priest." The priests who should have been setting an example were unable to rise above the level of the lowest man in society; that was true of the king also.

Unfortunately, we are living in a day in which our spiritual and political leadership is certainly not worthy of emulation. Liberalism is predominant in theology; liberalism is predominant in politics; and our news media are altogether liberal. Spiritual deterioration and decline in a nation will eventually bring it to destruction. That is what happened to Israel, and that nation furnishes a pattern for what can happen to us today.

And the revolters are profound to make slaughter, though I have been a rebuker of them all [Hos. 5:2].

God rebuked Israel for their brutality—there was murder, there was violence, and there was warfare. It is my conviction that the United States is today feeling the effects of God's judgment upon us. In Vietnam we fought perhaps the most disgraceful war that was ever fought, and we did so against the warnings of generals who said that we should never fight a land war in Asia. We made a terrible blunder by getting involved in that, and what has happened in that land is tragic. Did we help them? I think not, and the judgment of God is upon us and, actually, upon the white man. This has been called "the white man's day," and it certainly has been that. Earlier in history it was the sons of Ham who headed up the great pagan civilizations of Egypt, Babylon, and Assyria. However, it is the sons of Japheth, the white man, who has made the greatest blunder of all, and that is this: We have had the Word of God, the Bible, and we have not sent missionaries as we should have done. We did too little in getting the Word of God out to China, and God closed the door—I say *God*, not communism, closed the door. We did not send Bibles to Vietnam; we sent bullets and bombs over there. Because we did not send men to give out the Word of God, we had to send boys to die on the battlefield. We ought to wake up today to the fact that we cannot take God to the end of His universe and dismiss Him and tell Him we do not need Him anymore. We are feeling the effects of His judgment upon us, just as Israel did.

> **I know Ephraim, and Israel is not hid from me: for now, O Ephraim, thou committest whoredom, and Israel is defiled.**

> **They will not frame their doings to turn unto their God: for the spirit of whoredoms is in the midst of them, and they have not known the LORD [Hos. 5:3–4].**

I have said previously that I think "Ephraim" is a pet name that God chose for the nation Israel. Although it was the name of just one of the tribes, He used it to represent all ten of the northern tribes. But I think there is a second reason that God chose Ephraim to represent all of the northern kingdom: Ephraim was the very center of idolatry in Israel. The first golden calf was set up by Jeroboam in Bethel; later on, a second one was set up in Samaria. Both of these places were in the tribe of Ephraim—Bethel was probably in the tribe of Benjamin, but that area revolted with Ephraim and the rest of the northern kingdom. Ephraim was the very heart of idolatry, and idolatry was the great sin of the nation Israel.

"I know Ephraim, and Israel is not hid from me: for now, O Ephraim, thou committest whoredom, and Israel is defiled." God knows what He is talking about. Although the calf worship, or the worship of Baal, had been set up in the tribe of Ephraim, it had defiled all ten of the tribes and even had had its effect upon the southern kingdom. Their sin was the sin of a people who had the Word of God and who knew God but had turned from Him and no longer knew Him or worshiped Him. As a result, gross immorality and deterioration set in throughout every part of the nation, affecting even the ecology of the nation. God said that even the land and the animals were affected, and I think the curse of God is still upon that land today. What little irrigation has been done has not yet made the ". . . desert . . . blossom as the rose" (Isa. 35:1).

> **And the pride of Israel doth testify to his face: therefore shall Israel and Ephraim fall in their iniquity; Judah also shall fall with them [Hos. 5:5].**

God is saying that all ten tribes will be conquered, and "Judah also shall fall with them," but He does not say, "at the same time." However, Judah was finally brought down, and both of these kingdoms were carried away into captivity. The northern kingdom was carried into captivity by Assyria; about a century later, the southern kingdom was taken to Babylon. From that captivity there has never actually been the return to the land which the Word of God speaks about. This Book of Hosea makes it abundantly clear that when God brings them back, the *world* will know it, and there will be peace in the land.

> **They shall go with their flocks and with their herds to seek the LORD; but they shall not find him; he hath withdrawn himself from them [Hos. 5:6].**

In other words, the people have deserted God, but when trouble comes upon them and after they have tried every other resource, they will turn to God. God is their last resource, but they will not find Him because He has withdrawn Himself from them.

For many people, turning to God is the last resort. There is told the story of a ship which was crossing the Atlantic years ago, and the ship hit an iceberg. The captain sent out the order all over the ship. "To prayers, to prayers!" One woman on board the ship came rushing up to the captain and said, "Captain, has it come to this?" She was implying that if they were going to pray, they had come to the last resort. That is the way many people treat God. To them He is like a spare tire which they have on hand but are always hoping they won't have to use. Or He is like a life insurance policy or a fire extinguisher—you hope you never have to use them but they are there just in case the emergency arises.

They have dealt treacherously against the LORD: for they have begotten strange children: now shall a month devour them with their portions [Hos. 5:7].

"For they have begotten strange children"—that is, they are strange to God. The people did not bring up their children in the nurture and admonition of the Lord, in the discipline and instruction of the Lord. Back in the Book of Deuteronomy God told His people that they were to be continually teaching His Word to their children. They were to put it on the doorposts and teach it as they sat in their homes and as they walked together and even when they were going to bed at night. But now He says, "You have begotten *strange* children—they don't even know Me."

Blow ye the cornet in Gibeah, and the trumpet in Ramah: cry aloud at Beth-aven, after thee, O Benjamin [Hos. 5:8].

"Beth-aven" is Bethel. That part of the tribe of Benjamin had apparently revolted with the northern kingdom. God is saying here that the word of warning is to go out over all the land and to all the people.

Ephraim shall be desolate in the day of rebuke: among the tribes of Israel have I made known that which shall surely be [Hos. 5:9].

In other words, God had not failed to warn the people. He had warned them, He had rebuked them, and they still would not hear.

The princes of Judah were like them that remove the bound: therefore I will pour out my wrath upon them like water [Hos. 5:10].

The southern kingdom had apparently attempted to move its bound-
aries as far north as it possibly could, and there evidently was a real
division caused by the fact that the two nations could not agree on the
boundary. God had a message through Hosea for the southern kingdom as well, although he primarily was a prophet to the northern
kingdom.

> **Ephraim is oppressed and broken in judgment, because
> he willingly walked after the commandment [Hos.
> 5:11].**

Ephraim willingly followed the idols and the worship of idols—he
went with the crowd.

> **Therefore will I be unto Ephraim as a moth, and to the
> house of Judah as rottenness [Hos. 5:12].**

The prophets use figures of speech which are quite interesting. There
is great profit in studying the prophets, if I may make a play on words,
because they reach out into nature and use certain figures of speech
which are helpful to us in understanding the Word of God. "Therefore
will I be unto Ephraim as a moth." What does a moth do? A moth can
get into your closet, and if you do not have mothballs in there, it can
ruin a suit of clothes. The story is told about the man who had bought
some mothballs at a drugstore but brought them back, saying they
didn't work. When the druggist asked him what he meant, the man
said, "I stayed up half the night throwing these balls at the moths, but
I never hit one of them!" My friend, moths are something you do not
want in your closet, because in just one night they can ruin a very
valuable wool garment. God says, "I am going to be to Ephraim like a
moth; I will judge him in a hurry."

"And to the house of Judah as rottenness." It takes a wooden board
or a wooden foundation of a house a long time to become rotten. God
has said to Ephraim, the northern kingdom, "I'm going to judge you
now. However, in the southern kingdom rottenness is also setting in,

and, finally, it will collapse—but it will take longer for that to take place."

Our foundations are being removed in every way imaginable in our nation today, and rottenness has already begun in that which is left. It may take a while, my friend, but we cannot continue in sin like we are and expect to escape God's judgment. The situation is enough to make us weep today.

> **When Ephraim saw his sickness, and Judah saw his wound, then went Ephraim to the Assyrian, and sent to king Jareb: yet could he not heal you, nor cure you of your wound [Hos. 5:13].**

"When Ephraim saw his sickness"—Ephraim was sick, sick nigh unto death. "And Judah saw his wound"—Judah was hurt at this time also, because Assyria had come against them but did not take them into captivity.

"Then went Ephraim to the Assyrian, and sent to king Jareb: yet could he not heal you, nor cure you of your wound." Ephraim went to a quack doctor. They thought that the king of Assyria would help them, but he is the one who took them into captivity—they appealed for help to the wrong one.

> **For I will be unto Ephraim as a lion, and as a young lion to the house of Judah: I, even I, will tear and go away; I will take away, and none shall rescue him [Hos. 5:14].**

Here is another marvelous figure of speech. God says, "To Ephraim I am going to be as a lion, but to the southern kingdom I am going to be a young lion, a lion cub." The other evening I was watching on television a nature picture about lions. It showed how the mother lion protects her cubs. One of those little fellows looked just like a great big roly-poly cat—I wished I could have one as a pet. But that mother lion was vicious, especially when another animal would come near her cubs. She would really go after that animal, and the little cubs would just keep on playing. God said to the northern kingdom that He was going to be a lion—He intended to destroy them. To the southern kingdom He was going to be just a lion cub. But what happens to a lion cub? He grows up and some day is just as vicious as his mama. This was a warning to the southern kingdom that some day judgment was coming to them also.

"I, even I, will tear and go away; I will take away, and none shall rescue him." God was going to let Ephraim go into captivity, and they could whine and cry all they wanted to, but He would not rescue them. God judged their sin.

God judges sin even today—no one is really getting by with it. We have failed our young people today. Venereal disease is in epidemic stages, and we say, "What in the world is happening?" I'll tell you what is happening: God says you do not get by with *sin*—He is judging sin, and He will continue to judge sin, my friend.

I will go and return to my place, till they acknowledge their offence, and seek my face: in their affliction they will seek me early [Hos. 5:15].

Although this has been a doleful chapter entirely about judgment, it closes here with a note of hope. The time will come when Israel will again seek God, but He will not deliver them until they turn to Him.

CHAPTER 6

THEME: Israel will return in the last days; Israel presently to be judged for current sins

ISRAEL WILL RETURN IN THE LAST DAYS

Come, and let us return unto the Lord: for he hath torn, and he will heal us; he hath smitten, and he will bind us up [Hos. 6:1].

This is God's last call to the northern kingdom in that day, but it also looks to the future of that nation when God will heal them; although He has torn them, He intends to bind them up. This should be a warning that God will judge the sin of any nation that makes a profession of being a Christian nation and which has had the benefit of the Word of God.

After two days will he revive us: in the third day he will raise us up, and we shall live in his sight [Hos. 6:2].

"In the third day he will raise us up"—this is very interesting in light of the fact that the resurrection of Christ was on the third day. He was raised for the justification of both Jew and Gentile. This will also be applicable in that future day when God will bring Israel back into that land and bring them to Himself. In Ezekiel 37 God speaks of that day as a resurrection, and that resurrection will be based on the One who was raised on the third day; for in Christ's resurrection there is provided, for any man who will accept it, a redemption and a justification which will bring him into a right relationship with Almighty God.

The apostle Paul develops the subject of the future of Israel in Romans 11. In our day, God's purpose in building His church is to draw to Himself both Jew and Gentile, people out of every tongue and tribe and nation, who are going to come before Him to worship. When God completes His purpose in the church and takes it out of the world, He will again turn to the nation Israel and will raise her up. Every prophet who wrote in Scripture—and even some who didn't write—spoke of God's future purpose for the nation Israel. Even before the children of Israel could get into the land, Moses began to talk about the coming day when God would restore them back to the land for the third time. The third time—on the third day, so to speak—the restoration to the land would be a permanent restoration. There is a correlation between this restoration and Christ's being raised from the dead on the third day.

Then shall we know, if we follow on to know the LORD: his going forth is prepared as the morning; and he shall come unto us as the rain, as the latter and former rain unto the earth [Hos. 6:3].

"And he shall come unto us as the rain, as the latter and former rain unto the earth." The former rains were the heavy rains which fell toward the end of October, and the latter rains were the heavy showers of March and April which came right before the harvest. There are folk who say that the latter rain has returned to that land, but I do not think you can say that either the former or latter rain has returned. The rainfall in Israel is much less than we have in Southern California, and here it is not the rain which makes this area a so-called Garden of Eden (despite its smog and traffic); it is irrigation that makes the land productive. But in Israel there is not enough water to irrigate all the land, and we are not seeing the fulfillment of the promised return of the rains to that land. When these people again turn to God, however, the blessing will come not only to the people, but also to the land and the animal world.

"Then shall we know, if we follow on to know the LORD." That is the very secret of the solution to the problems of life—to know the Lord. The apostle Paul, even when he had come to the end of his life, had this ambition: "That I may know him [that is, the Lord Jesus Christ], and the power of his resurrection, and the fellowship of his sufferings, being made conformable unto his death" (Phil. 3:10).

There is no way for improvement in this life apart from a knowledge of God. The Word of God is very emphatic about that, and either it is right or it is wrong. Over thousands of years the Word of God has been proven right, and I do not think the present generation is upsetting it by any means.

ISRAEL PRESENTLY TO BE JUDGED
FOR CURRENT SINS

O Ephraim, what shall I do unto thee? O Judah, what shall I do unto thee? for your goodness is as a morning cloud, and as the early dew it goeth away [Hos. 6:4].

God sounds as if He is just a little bit frustrated here. In effect, He is saying, "What am I going to do with you? I love you, but you continue on in sin and I am going to have to judge you!" This puts God on the horns of a dilemma. Judgment is the strange work of God—He wants to *save*, not judge. But when people keep turning away from God, then the day comes when He has to judge them.

The people of Israel were religious, but they had no knowledge of God and were far from Him. We today have a lot of religion, and I am opposed to it. Let me illustrate my point with a letter which a man wrote to the editor of a newspaper:

> In today's society, religion has outlasted its usefulness. Man at long last has outgrown the necessity for this opiate. No longer does he have to explain the unknown with folktales and the worship of a superior being. In a complex society such as ours, religion can only mute and cloud the mind. Religion blurs and distorts important details and information, interferes with important decisions, and promotes bigotry and prejudice. Now is the time for humanity to discard this mental blindfold.

This may startle you, but I agree with what that man wrote; I wish that we could get rid of religion. Someone answered this letter, and his reply was also published. He expressed it so much better than I could:

In response to the April 26 letter entitled "Religion Termed Mental Blindfold," I agree with Mr. _____ about the effects of religion, for religion is man's attempt to reach God through his own efforts. I have never been a religious man, but about four years ago, something happened that has really changed my life. I invited Jesus Christ to take control of my life and accepted the fact that I cannot reach God by myself, but that He has made a relationship with Him possible through His Son Jesus Christ. Since that commitment, I have grown increasingly aware of my social responsibility and have grown to love and accept myself and other people regardless of age, race, creed, or color.

Today many are saying, "Out with religion," and I say, fine, let's sweep it out the back door, and let's invite Jesus Christ, the Light of the world, to come in.

The Israelites were religious, but their goodness was like "a morning cloud"—just form and ritual and ceremony. "As the early dew it goeth away"—that is all their religion amounted to. Many people wear religion like you would wear a loose-fitting garment; it is something they can put on or off at any time. God condemned these people because they were religious, but they did not know Him, and they had never had a transforming, life-changing, experience with Him.

Therefore have I hewed them by the prophets; I have slain them by the words of my mouth: and thy judgments are as the light that goeth forth [Hos. 6:5].

In other words, God says, "I skinned them alive by the prophets." I appreciate the many letters I receive that commend us for giving out the Word of God as it is, for hewing to the line and letting the chips fall where they may. I have always tried to do that throughout the years of my ministry, and I have found that the folk who sincerely want to hear the Word of God will appreciate it. Others will oppose it, and I expect to hear their criticism also. God says to His people here, "I've skinned you alive by the prophets—they have been faithful in telling it like it is—but you have not listened to them." And in our day, although there is a great interest in and turning to the Word of God, we wonder how much of it has really transformed the hearts and lives of those who hear.

"I have slain them by the words of my mouth: and thy judgments are as the light that goeth forth." They were not sinning because of *ignorance*—there was no lack of information. God had sent the prophets to them, but they had turned their backs on God and His Word.

> **For I desired mercy, and not sacrifice; and the knowledge of God more than burnt offerings [Hos. 6:6].**

The people were merely going through a form. My friend, you can go to church on Sunday and be as fundamental as you can be. You may criticize the preacher, criticize the choir, criticize everybody—maybe they deserve it, I don't know—but God's desire is that you put His Word into shoe leather, that you allow it to get down where the rubber meets the road, and that there be an evidence of *mercy* in your own heart and life. Don't think that going to a church banquet is somehow a substitute for truly eating the Bread of Life or of enjoying a big porterhouse steak from the Word of God. No church function is a substitute for really studying the Word of God.

> **But they like men have transgressed the covenant: there have they dealt treacherously against me [Hos. 6:7].**

"The covenant"—that is, the covenant which God had made with this nation.

> **Gilead is a city of them that work iniquity, and is polluted with blood [Hos. 6:8].**

The city of Gilead is best known to us for the ". . . *balm* in Gilead . . ." (Jer. 8:22, italics mine), which was an aromatic gum or resin used for medical purposes. However, in Hosea's day only iniquity came out of Gilead.

And as troops of robbers wait for a man, so the company of priests murder in the way by consent: for they commit lewdness [Hos. 6:9].

In other words, the priests in refusing to give the people the Water of Life and the Bread of Life were actually committing murder. To be honest with you, I think that a minister who stands in the pulpit and does not give out the Word of God is guilty just as it is stated right here. I did not think that up—it is the Word of God which says that.

I have seen an horrible thing in the house of Israel: there is the whoredom of Ephraim, Israel is defiled.

Also, O Judah, he hath set an harvest for thee, when I returned the captivity of my people [Hos. 6:10-11].

This is a warning to Judah that their day of judgment is also coming. "When I returned the captivity of my people"—there is a future day when God will bring the people back to the land, but at that time He had to judge them for their sin.

CHAPTER 7

THEME: Israel turns to Egypt and Assyria

Chapters 7—12 deal with the fact that Israel could escape judgment by turning to God who loves her. God is dealing with Israel in a harsh way; yet in tenderness He is attempting to call the people back to Himself before judgment comes.

Israel turns to Egypt and Assyria instead of turning to God.

ISRAEL TURNS TO EGYPT AND ASSYRIA

When I would have healed Israel, then the iniquity of Ephraim was discovered, and the wickedness of Samaria: for they commit falsehood; and the thief cometh in, and the troop of robbers spoileth without [Hos. 7:1].

Samaria was the capital of the northern kingdom—that is, Omri made it the capital, and then Ahab and Jezebel built a palace there.

On our recent trips to Israel I insisted that Samaria be included in the tour. I wanted the folk to go to that hill of Samaria and see the fulfillment of prophecy. The judgment of God is on what is probably one of the most beautiful spots in the world. It would be a lovely spot for a palace, or for that matter, for a home. From the top of the hill there is a view of the entire area. To the west is the Mediterranean Sea, to the east the Jordan Valley, to the north Mount Hermon and Megiddo, to the south the city of Jerusalem. It is a choice spot with nothing to obstruct the view in any direction. But today it is a desolate waste. Indeed the judgment of God is upon it.

What was happening in Israel during Hosea's day was that the sin which had been covered was being uncovered. That which they had been doing secretly they were now doing openly. There was no shame, no conviction, no conscience relative to their sin. The Lord would forgive their iniquity if they would repent and turn to Him. Instead, they persisted in their wickedness and went farther and farther into it.

It is one thing to sin in secret—that is bad enough—but it is even worse to bring your sin out in the open and flaunt it before the world. To do that is to sink to the very bottom. This is the reason that I believe Hosea has a message for my own nation as well as all other nations. Since the people of Israel were God's chosen people, and yet God sent them into captivity when they persisted in sinning against Him, does it seem likely that any other nation could get by with the same type of sin?

For example, when I was growing up in Nashville, Tennessee, the few homosexuals who lived there kept their homosexuality under cover. They operated rather secretly and concealed their sin. However, now across the country they are very open about their perversion and are demanding acceptance and protection of their activity. The fact is being uncovered that there are not only call girls but call boys and that homosexuals are numbered in the thousands. What was formerly done in secret is now brought out into the open, and this is characteristic of other sins as well.

Someone said to me just recently, "Dr. McGee, in our day people sinned just as they do today."

"Yes, they did," I agreed. "Before I was saved, I was with that crowd, and I know."

"Well, then, what's the difference?"

"I'll tell you the difference. In my day we kept it under the cover. There was still some shame connected with sin. Today sin is brought out in the open and is flaunted before the world." It is called a new morality, and actually a sort of halo is put around sin today. The sinner is commended for doing something new and daring and courageous. The other day I heard a girl complimented as being honest and courageous because she was living with a man to whom she was not married and had an illegitimate child. Well, I am a square, I know (as someone said, being a square keeps me from going around in circles), but we must face the fact that God's Word has not changed. The openness of sin is not a mark of advancement, but it indicates that we are losing the civilization which formerly carried some semblance of Christian culture.

And they consider not in their hearts that I remember all their wickedness: now their own doings have beset them about; they are before my face [Hos. 7:2].

God is saying, "I knew about their sins before, but now they have taken a further step away from Me and are doing their sinning out in the open." In other words, they have now reached the lowest depths of immorality.

They make the king glad with their wickedness, and the princes with their lies [Hos. 7:3].

The king and the princes applauded this sort of behavior. In our day it is tragic when the leadership in any field—education, science, politics, or the church—give themselves over to foul and blasphemous language, as they are now doing. That is something else that is out in the open. A foulmouthed leader is applauded as being a he-man. Well, it also indicates that he has a very poor vocabulary and is not able to express himself. Unfortunately, this verse is applicable to our nation, and history tells us that it has been applicable to great nations in the past that have now passed off the stage of human events and lie in rubble, covered by the dust of the centuries.

They are all adulterers, as an oven heated by the baker, who ceaseth from raising after he hath kneaded the dough, until it be leavened [Hos. 7:4].

This figure of speech is tremendous. The baker had his oven ready but didn't bring up the heat until the dough was kneaded and ready to bake. Here God is not talking about spiritual adultery but about gross immorality. They had formerly kept their sin under cover, but now they are like an open oven, hot with passion. In our day I get the impression that men are trying to prove that they are virile and women are trying to prove that they are sexually alert. In modern America there is a tremendous open obsession with sex.

In the day of our king the princes have made him sick with bottles of wine; he stretched out his hand with scorners [Hos. 7:5].

The king has become an alcoholic, and he is making a fool of himself. We have mentioned this before, but it is so important that we will keep repeating it. What was it that brought down the northern kingdom? It was idolatry, a turning away from God. That will always manifest itself in gross immorality. Wine and women, the bottle and the brothel, sauce and sex are the things that occupied the attention of the northern kingdom.

Now if you think I am a square or unfair or a bigot, will you let me ask you a fair question? As you look about you today, what is the chief occupation of men and women in all walks of life? Isn't it an occupation with liquor and with sex? Haven't these two become the prominent things in this civilization of ours? Isn't it true that it is being brought out in the open today as never before in our country? When these sins were brought out in the open in Israel, God said that He would have to move and judge them.

For they have made ready their heart like an oven, whiles they lie in wait: their baker sleepeth all the night; in the morning it burneth as a flaming fire [Hos. 7:6].

Everything is done to stir up the passions of men and women. In our day we hear this so-called sophisticated argument about pornography: "We are adults and should have the right to choose what we want to see and what we want to hear." Well, there isn't much freedom to choose what we want to see and what we want to hear when we are bombarded with filth everywhere we turn. I don't have the liberty to choose what is presented on television or the radio or the advertising media. I think there are a great many people who would like to see better things and hear better things than are presented to us today, but that freedom is denied us in order that the other crowd can have their freedom to give themselves over to sin.

They are all hot as an oven, and have devoured their judges; all their kings are fallen: there is none among them that calleth unto me [Hos. 7:7].

"All their kings are fallen." The northern kingdom did not have one good king. If you were to look back in the historical books and go through the list of the kings of Israel and Judah, you would note that Judah had a few good kings—in fact, five kings of Judah led in revivals—but the northern kingdom didn't have a good king in the lot. Every king was as wicked as he could be. Ahab and Jezebel reached the bottom of the list, but some of the others would run them a close second.

Many of the kings in the northern kingdom were assassinated. They made nine different changes of dynasty in their short history. The kings in the northern kingdom started off with Jeroboam, but you don't get very far into the story until someone gets in and murders his line. Another line of kings starts out, and it doesn't go very far until someone else is murdered. Several of the kings had a short reign, and their sons didn't even make it to the throne. That was a judgment of God upon them. You see, God had chosen and promised to bless the line of David; He made no such promise to the kings of the divided kingdom in the north.

Ephraim, he hath mixed himself among the people; Ephraim is a cake not turned [Hos. 7:8].

"Ephraim, he hath mixed himself among the people." God never goes in for mixtures. Have you noted that? He seems to want His children to stay in their own crowd.

"Ephraim is a cake not turned." Here we go again with another good, homely illustration, and Hosea has many of them. What does he mean? In that day they cooked on the top of a stove and made little cakes like our pancakes. They still make those kind of cakes there today. Now you know that a pancake that is not turned can be burned on the one side and raw on the other. That is the picture of Ephraim. The nation was hot on one side but raw on the other side.

They blew hot and cold toward God. There is a whimsical little story told of a man who had been wandering through the woods and came up to a cottage. The man who lived in the cottage invited him into his home. As the man came in out of the cold, he began to blow on his hands. "Why do you blow on your hands?" asked the host. "To make them warm," answered the wanderer. Then the host offered the visitor a bowl of hot soup. The man began to blow on the soup. "Why do you blow on the soup?" asked the host. "To make it cool," answered the guest. So the host jumped up and ran out of his own house, saying, "I don't like anybody who can blow hot and cold!" Well, my friend, that is the way a great many people are as far as Christianity is concerned. With one crowd they blow hot and with another crowd they blow cold. They are like Ephraim—a cake (a pancake) not turned.

Strangers have devoured his strength, and he knoweth it not: yea, gray hairs are here and there upon him, yet he knoweth not.

And the pride of Israel testifieth to his face: and they do not return to the Lord their God, nor seek him for all this.

Ephraim also is like a silly dove without heart: they call to Egypt, they go to Assyria [Hos. 7:9–11].

This is another interesting illustration. If you have ever been dove hunting, you know that if a dove has a nest with eggs or little ones in it she will act as if she has a broken wing and actually let you get very close to her. She tries to lure you away from her nest. Actually, that is not a very smart move on the part of the dove for two reasons. When a dove lets you get that close to her, you know there is a nest nearby. Secondly, she endangers her own life.

Now here was Ephraim. She refused to run to God for help. So first she ran down to Egypt for help. When Egypt wouldn't give her the help she wanted, she went up to Assyria and asked for help. She went back and forth like a silly dove. What a picture!

When they shall go, I will spread my net upon them; I will bring them down as the fowls of the heaven; I will chastise them, as their congregation hath heard [Hos. 7:12].

I can remember as a boy that we would get a big box, prop up one end, and put corn under it. We would have the corn lead right under the box. We would hide in the barn, and the doves would come to eat the corn. They would follow the corn right under the box. Then we would pull a string, and the box would come down on them. Silly doves. That is what God says here. He will spread His net upon them. They will be caught.

Woe unto them! for they have fled from me: destruction unto them! because they have transgressed against me: though I have redeemed them, yet they have spoken lies against me [Hos. 7:13].

God had a redemption for them, and yet these people were continuing to turn from the living and true God.

And they have not cried unto me with their heart, when they howled upon their beds: they assemble themselves for corn and wine, and they rebel against me [Hos. 7:14].

They didn't realize that the famine they were having was a judgment of God upon them. They were crying about having no food.

Though I have bound and strengthened their arms, yet do they imagine mischief against me.

> **They return, but not to the most High: they are like a
> deceitful bow: their princes shall fall by the sword for
> the rage of their tongue: this shall be their derision in
> the land of Egypt [Hos. 7:15–16].**

"They are like a deceitful bow." You put an arrow in it to shoot at
something and the string breaks. It is a deceitful bow—you can't depend upon it.

"This shall be their derision in the land of Egypt." He is saying that
Egypt will begin to mock them and ridicule them for the way they are
acting.

You can see that this is a very severe section of the Word of God.
Hosea was not the most popular prophet in his day. He wouldn't be a
popular prophet today, either. However, he still has a message for us,
and we do well to listen.

CHAPTER 8

THEME: Israel turns to golden calves and altars of sin

All of the prophets had not only a local message but also one that reaches into the future even beyond us today. However, their message does have an application for us. There are no prophecies more applicable to us than those of Hosea and Jeremiah. Each of these prophets prophesied right at the time of the downfall of this nation. Their messages ought to alarm us as a nation today, but I do not have the faith that they will. I am afraid that we may have stepped over the line and that judgment is inevitable, just as it was for Israel.

ISRAEL TURNS TO GOLDEN CALVES
AND ALTARS OF SIN

As Israel turned from God, they looked to their king and their wealth to deliver them—

> **Set the trumpet to thy mouth. He shall come as an eagle against the house of the LORD, because they have transgressed my covenant, and trespassed against my law.**
>
> **Israel shall cry unto me, My God, we know thee.**
>
> **Israel hath cast off the thing that is good: the enemy shall pursue him.**
>
> **They have set up kings, but not by me: they have made princes, and I knew it not: of their silver and their gold have they made them idols, that they may be cut off [Hos. 8:1-4].**

"Because they have transgressed my covenant, and trespassed against my law"—God is explaining why He is going to send them into captivity. Previously He spelled out their sins and showed that they had broken His commandments, but their sins had also resulted in their breaking the covenant which God had made with them. God had made a covenant with Abraham which was applicable to them, and He had made a covenant with Moses which was applicable to them, especially as it pertained to that land and how He would bless them in the land; but if they did not serve Him He would put them out of the land. And then God also made a covenant with David. Now the people had broken these covenants, but God will never break them. The covenant which God made with Abraham and the covenant which He made with David were both unconditional (the Mosaic covenant was conditional). The people could transgress the covenant, and when they did they were judged. They were put out of the land, but that has never altered the fact that God will give them that land for an eternal possession. It simply means that that generation was put out of the land, but another generation will be brought back. That is what happened when they came out of Egypt. Since the people would not enter the land because of their unbelief, God said they would never enter the land but that their children would inhabit it.

"They have set up kings, but not by me." God had said that the line of David was to rule over Israel. Jeroboam led a rebellion, and the line of kings which he set up did not include men who turned to the living God. These kings never attempted in any way to bring the people into the worship of God. Instead, they all went into idolatry. Jeroboam, at the very beginning, put up those two golden calves—one in Samaria and one in Bethel—and he did that to keep the people from returning to Jerusalem in the south to worship in the temple. God judged them because they had set up kings of whom He did not approve.

Thy calf, O Samaria, hath cast thee off; mine anger is kindled against them: how long will it be ere they attain to innocency? [Hos. 8:5].

"How long will it be ere they attain to innocency?" They were guilty, they were sinful, they were not innocent at all.

"Thy calf, O Samaria." Samaria had become the capital of Israel under Omri, the father of Ahab. Ahab married Jezebel whose father was a priest in Sidon among the Phoenicians, worshipers of Baal. Jezebel had transported to Israel several hundred prophets of Baal, and many Israelites became worshipers of Baal.

"Mine anger is kindled against them"—God intended to judge them. Samaria is a desolate place even today. I insisted on taking our tour group to see it. Though it is a beautiful spot, the desolation there is appalling; you cannot help but be overwhelmed by it. But there were once palaces of ivory in Samaria. The archaeologists say that they have found very lovely ivory perfume bottles and all kinds of beautiful ivory bric-a-brac in the ruins there. I noticed that the people on our tour were depressed after viewing the ruins, and rightly so. God has judged Samaria. It was a beautiful spot with lovely buildings, but God's judgment came upon it because the people had turned from Him and were worshiping the calf there.

For from Israel was it also: the workman made it; therefore it is not God: but the calf of Samaria shall be broken in pieces [Hos. 8:6].

I do not know where you would find that golden calf today. The archaeologists certainly have not found any piece of it there. It was probably taken somewhere and broken to pieces, maybe even melted down. God says to these people, "You have turned from Me to worship this, but it is not God and it is not able to help you."

For they have sown the wind, and they shall reap the whirlwind: it hath no stalk: the bud shall yield no meal: if so be it yield, the strangers shall swallow it up [Hos. 8:7].

This verse speaks of the judgment both of famine and of the enemy who was to come into that land.

Israel is swallowed up: now shall they be among the Gentiles as a vessel wherein is no pleasure [Hos. 8:8].

"Israel is swallowed up." Do you know where the ten tribes are today? So many people have the idea that the United States is the tribe of Ephraim—I cannot think of anything more absurd. If you think that is true, read these chapters here about God's judgment on Ephraim; nothing but judgment is mentioned of Ephraim.

"Now shall they be among the Gentiles as a vessel wherein is no pleasure." We are not able to locate or identify the tribes of Israel today. I am confident that the people of Israel mixed with the tribe of Judah when they returned to the land after their captivity, and there has been no way to separate them since that time. They are scattered throughout the world today. Actually, there are more Jews in New York City than there are in the whole nation of Israel; there are at least four times as many outside of the land than are in Israel today.

For they are gone up to Assyria, a wild ass alone by himself: Ephraim hath hired lovers [Hos. 8:9].

Here is another specific action which brought God's judgment upon Israel. What a condemnation this is! They are like one of these long-eared donkeys. Israel went up to Assyria for help and tried to buy off Assyria—"Ephraim hath hired lovers."

However, they found they could not buy off Assyria. Instead God would use Assyria to judge them—

Yea, though they have hired among the nations, now will I gather them, and they shall sorrow a little for the burden of the king of princes.

Because Ephraim hath made many altars to sin, altars shall be unto him to sin [Hos. 8:10–11].

An altar is a place of worship, and God had given Israel an altar. We see in the Book of Hebrews that the church has a heavenly altar; the throne of God is today a throne of grace to us, and the Lord Jesus is our Great High Priest at that altar making intercession for us. An altar is to be a place of worship, but here God says, "Because Ephraim hath made many altars to sin, altars shall be unto him to sin." Israel had turned to religion, to the worship of idols. It did not help them and only brought judgment upon them.

My friend, religion has been the most damning thing this world has ever experienced. Religion has damned the world. Look at India today where they cannot eat steak because the cows are sacred; there are multitudes starving to death, and yet they will not use cattle for food. Look at the conditions of China today or at our ancestors yonder in the wilderness of England. Throughout history religion has not helped us but has crippled and damned the human race. Only the Lord Jesus can deliver us.

I have written to him the great things of my law, but they were counted as a strange thing [Hos. 8:12].

"But they were counted as a strange thing"—that is, the people did not know anything about God's law. I say this often because there are so few who are saying it at all. God is saying here, "I have given them My written Word, and to them it is a strange thing—they are *ignorant* of it." That was the condemnation of Israel and, my friend, that is the condemnation of our nation today. We try to pass as a civilized, Christian nation, and we are anything but that. The ignorance of the Word of God is to me one of the most amazing things in this land. That is the reason we are committed to teaching the Bible. The most important business the church has is to get out the Word of God. I do not think your pastor is to be a business administrator. I do not think he is called to be a social lion who mixes and mingles with people. The important thing is whether he gives out the Word of God when he stands in that pulpit. If he does, then you should stand behind him. But I do not ask you to support a man who is playing around and riding the fence in liberalism. Across this land there are many men who are teaching the Word of God, and they are the ones who are getting a hearing today. However, their ministries and the ministry of a Bible teaching radio program like ours are just a drop in the bucket—this nation is ignorant of the Word of God.

> **They sacrifice flesh for the sacrifices of mine offerings, and eat it; but the LORD accepteth them not, now will he remember their iniquity, and visit their sins: they shall return to Egypt [Hos. 8:13].**

They go through the ceremony, they've got the ritual, and they know the vocabulary, but that is all it is. The Lord knows them and He doesn't accept them. I discovered as a pastor that you have a few people who learn the vocabulary of fundamentalism; they know when to say, "Praise the Lord" and "the Lord bless you." Those are wonderful expressions, but in the mouths of some people they are meaningless. "The Lord accepteth them not."

"Now will he remember their iniquity, and visit their sins: they shall return to Egypt." It is evident that when Babylon destroyed Assyria, many from the ten tribes joined with the ones who were taken into Babylonian captivity from Judah and returned to the land. Also, we know from the Book of Jeremiah that at the time of the Babylonian captivity many of the people went into Egypt. I believe that that is what Hosea is speaking of here, but there are many fine Bible expositors who would not agree with me.

> **For Israel hath forgotten his Maker, and buildeth temples; and Judah hath multiplied fenced cities: but I will send a fire upon his cities, and it shall devour the palaces thereof [Hos. 8:14].**

"For Israel hath forgotten his Maker, and buildeth temples." They had tried to build substitutes for the temple in Jerusalem. It was in that temple and in that temple *only* that God had said sacrifices were to be made to Him. "And Judah hath multiplied fenced cities"—Judah had sinned also, and God will judge them later. The thing that is going to happen first is that these temples in Israel are to be destroyed. It is interesting that the northern section of Israel seems to be more desolate than any other section of that land. Way down in the Negeb where they don't get any rain, you expect it to be that way, but up in the northern section—especially in the valley of Esdraelon, which is one of the richest valleys in the world—you do not expect the desolation which is there. Yet all around, even to this day, you see evidences of the judgment of God which came upon that land.

CHAPTER 9

THEME: Israel turns to land productivity

At this time Israel was beginning to look to prosperity as the indication that everything was all right in the nation. In other words, they were trying to increase the value of their money, and they were attempting to increase the production of the land. But God said that they were nothing but a backsliding heifer. He had blessed them with prosperity, and that had blinded them to the reality of their spiritual condition. In fact, they are right on the verge of captivity, which was the judgment of God.

> **Rejoice not, O Israel, for joy, as other people: for thou hast gone a-whoring from thy God, thou hast loved a reward upon every cornfloor [Hos. 9:1].**

"Rejoice not, O Israel, for joy, as other people"—they were sinning more and enjoying it less.

"For thou hast gone a-whoring from thy God." God says, "You have played the harlot."

"Thou hast loved a reward upon every cornfloor." In other words, Israel was trying to increase their production, but instead it became a judgment upon them. The stock market was up, and there was abundance. The shelves of the supermarket were groaning with food; there was plenty of liquor to be bought, plenty of wine, all of which deceived Israel.

Our nation today has also been deceived by prosperity. We are finding out that these great big combines, these large corporations, are probably not the blessing that we thought at one time they would be. Even farming is often done by large corporations. However, the important thing today is the stock market. Certainly the stock market is more important to our nation than are the Scriptures. That was what was happening in Israel—there was a false prosperity in the land, and they were far from dependent upon God.

I believe that one of the methods God has used to judge the United States is that He has judged us with prosperity. After World War II, I predicted that we were going to have to suffer as the other nations had suffered during the war. We did not have any bombing as did England, France, Germany, and Japan. We escaped all that, but I felt at the time that God would judge us somehow. After the war we became the most prosperous nation in the world, and it seemed a contradiction of the statements I was making. It took me about ten years to see what God was doing. God judged us with prosperity, and that is what He did to Israel. He said, "I have provided everything for you, and you're giving credit to your own ingenuity and your own ability. You're a proud people, and you're not looking to Me nor giving Me credit at all." That is the picture of Israel and, my friend, that just happens to be a picture of my nation since World War II.

The floor and the winepress shall not feed them, and the new wine shall fail in her [Hos. 9:2].

In other words, there is going to be scarcity rather than abundance.

They shall not dwell in the LORD's land; but Ephraim shall return to Egypt, and they shall eat unclean things in Assyria [Hos. 9:3].

"They shall not dwell in the LORD's land." God makes it clear that He is going to put them out of the land. Although He said He would never forget His covenants with Abraham, Moses, and David, Israel's tenure in the land always depended on their obedience to God. Now He is going to put them out of the land.

"And they shall eat unclean things in Assyria." The people had been turning from God and breaking His law. Now God says, "I'm really going to give you a diet of unclean things." They are not going to have any more fun—they were sinning more, but enjoying it less. I am of the opinion that that is true of a great many people today. I talked once with a man in some meetings in the East, who said to me, "The reason I came tonight, Dr. McGee, is that I've tried everything in this world, and I am *so* sick of sin, just sick of it." He was sinning more, but enjoying it less, and that was what finally brought that man to Christ.

> **They shall not offer wine offerings to the Lord, neither shall they be pleasing unto him: their sacrifices shall be unto them as the bread of mourners; all that eat thereof shall be polluted: for their bread for their soul shall not come into the house of the Lord.**
>
> **What will ye do in the solemn day, and in the day of the feast of the Lord?**
>
> **For, lo, they are gone because of destruction: Egypt shall gather them up, Memphis shall bury them: the pleasant places for their silver, nettles shall possess them: thorns shall be in their tabernacles [Hos. 9:4–6].**

Many of them went down into the land of Egypt following the captivity. Out of the land, they could not worship God as He intended them to.

> **The days of visitation are come, the days of recompence are come; Israel shall know it: the prophet is a fool, the spiritual man is mad, for the multitude of thine iniquity, and the great hatred [Hos. 9:7].**

Israel had lost its way spiritually. Why? Because of the leadership.

When I started out to study for the ministry, the big debate in the church in this country was between what was then known as fundamentalism and modernism. Modernism espoused the social gospel. They were the do-gooders, and they claimed they had a high ethical standard. Frankly, I was inclined to agree with them because I found that many fundamentalists didn't operate on high ethics. It disturbed me a great deal to think that the liberals had one strike on us in that connection. But I watched them carefully and found that they didn't really have a high ethical standard. Hosea said it, and you can blame it on him; he said, "The prophet is a fool."

For example, there was a young man who attended Yale and had there an outstanding liberal preacher who taught ethics. This preacher taught young men to burn their draft cards—and that's against the law. In certain protest meetings he taught and espoused that there is a higher law than the law of the land. The young man heard these things and thought, *Well, if that's ethics, then I will follow that.* He was led into very serious trouble because of such teaching.

May I say to you, liberalism has lost even its moral standard today. I was in Portland, Oregon, at the time it was discovered through the testimony of a policewoman that the place where the young people were getting narcotics was run by the liberal churches. Hosea said, "The prophet is a fool"—he has led the nation astray.

Liberalism is also responsible for the policy this nation followed after World War II, and the trouble we are in today is a trouble that has been produced by liberalism. I will say this, fundamentalism may act fanatically at times, but the fact of the matter is that fundamentalism did not lead this country into the trouble we are in today. Before I even entered seminary I listened to men like Dr. Harry Ironside, Dr. Harry Rimmer, and Dr. Arthur Brown, and I heard my liberal professors and preachers call them fanatics. But what those men said and preached is true today, and the things I was taught by those liberal professors are not true at all—it just didn't work out the way they said.

Israel had turned their backs on God, and judgment was coming because of it. They had no spiritual discernment. It is the ignorance of the Word of God that disturbs me about our nation today. We receive many letters from people who are coming out of various cults and "isms"—and we rejoice in that—but how did they get trapped in all of these groups? There is only one explanation: ignorance of the Word of God and lack of spiritual discernment. God said that He intended to judge Israel, and that should be an illustration to any nation which makes a pretense of being a Christian nation.

> **The watchman of Ephraim was with my God: but the prophet is a snare of a fowler in all his ways, and hatred in the house of his God [Hos. 9:8].**

"The watchman of Ephraim was with my God"—evidently there were a few fanatical fundamentalists around in that day warning the people of the coming judgment.

"But the prophet is a snare of a fowler." That is harsh language, and I would never use that kind of language to speak of the liberal today. However, I do believe that liberalism is in control in my day, especially over the news media. They have sacred cows known as freedom of the press and freedom of speech, but they allow the fundamentalists very little freedom, I can assure you of that. Liberalism—whether it is in politics, the news media, or in the pulpit—is a snare; it is like a trap, and it brainwashes people. As a result, this nation has been in trouble ever since World War II. It is time someone made the diagnosis and gave the prognosis of the case: the problem is that we have turned from God as a nation. God has become a big swear word in Washington, D.C. His name is often used in the form of blasphemy but seldom in the form of prayer or in worship of Him.

> **They have deeply corrupted themselves, as in the days of Gibeah: therefore he will remember their iniquity, he will visit their sins [Hos. 9:9].**

There are no ifs, ands, or buts about it—God intends to judge sin. Maybe you don't like it, but that is what He says: He intends to judge sin.

> **I found Israel like grapes in the wilderness; I saw your fathers as the first-ripe in the fig tree at her first time: but they went to Baal-peor, and separated themselves unto that shame; and their abominations were according as they loved [Hos. 9:10].**

The vine and the fig tree are symbols of the nation Israel which are used throughout the Word of God.

Israel not only established calf worship in both Samaria and Bethel, but, under Ahab and Jezebel, they also brought in the prophets of Baal.

> **As for Ephraim, their glory shall fly away like a bird, from the birth, and from the womb, and from the conception [Hos. 9:11].**

Have you ever been duck hunting and spent the cold hours of the morning in a duck trap or in a boat out on the lake? Then right before the sun comes up and you can finally start shooting, someone else out there fires a gun, and every duck on the lake and anywhere nearby takes off! You just sit there and watch them fly away. That is the picture of the glory of Ephraim—it was departing. This nation had made a tremendous impact upon the ancient world, but its glory was flying away like a bird.

> **Though they bring up their children, yet will I bereave them, that there shall not be a man left: yea, woe also to them when I depart from them! [Hos. 9:12].**

This is another judgment which God was going to bring upon them. God had promised Abraham not only to give him the land but also to multiply his seed. God had said that Abraham's seed would be like the sand on the seashore and like the stars in the heavens. God made good that promise, but now the people have sinned and He says, "You're going to have a real decline in your birthrate as part of My judgment upon you."

"Not be a man left" is not a declaration that God would completely wipe out the population, but that there would be no man left who would stand for God.

> Ephraim, as I saw Tyrus, is planted in a pleasant place:
> but Ephraim shall bring forth his children to the mur-
> derer [Hos. 9:13].

"Tyrus" is Tyre. God had not yet judged Tyre, and it was at that time a
great commercial center. Its prosperity was like a fever, and it had
caught on in the northern kingdom which also became a commercial
center. There was a false prosperity in the land, and the people were
deceived by it.

> Give them, O LORD: what wilt thou give? give them a
> miscarrying womb and dry breasts [Hos. 9:14].

Their women were barren. It was the judgment of God upon them.

> All their wickedness is in Gilgal: for there I hated them:
> for the wickedness of their doings I will drive them out
> of mine house, I will love them no more: all their
> princes are revolters [Hos. 9:15].

In other words, God says to them, "Their sin in Gilgal brought My
judgment upon them, although I loved them. This should be a warning to you. I will judge you again, and you will come to the conclusion that I do not love you anymore."

> Ephraim is smitten, their root is dried up, they shall
> bear no fruit: yea, though they bring forth, yet will I slay
> even the beloved fruit of their womb [Hos. 9:16].

God's judgment was to come not only upon the fruit of the ground, but
also on the birth of children.

> My God will cast them away, because they did not hear-
> ken unto him: and they shall be wanderers among the
> nations [Hos. 9:17].

God says that He intends to cast them out and that they would be "wanderers among the nations." The ten tribes as such did not return after the captivity. It is true that they came back with Judah as a mixture, and they spread throughout the land. In fact, we find Joseph and Mary who were members of the tribe of Judah living way up in Galilee. There was a tremendous scattering even in the land when they returned after the Babylonian captivity, so that today most Jews could not tell you to which tribe they belong.

CHAPTER 10

THEME: Israel will become an empty vine

We are in a section in which God pronounces His judgment upon Israel. In this chapter we discover something else that Israel was doing which would bring God's judgment upon her.

ISRAEL WILL BECOME AN EMPTY VINE

Israel is an empty vine, he bringeth forth fruit unto himself: according to the multitude of his fruit he hath increased the altars; according to the goodness of his land they have made goodly images [Hos. 10:1].

He was not saying that Israel was a vine which was not producing fruit, because during this period Israel was very prosperous. God was still being good to them, although He was warning them of coming judgment. "He bringeth forth fruit unto himself" means that he was a vine that was emptying itself of its fruit—just pouring out fruit upon the people. You see, although God had made Israel prosperous, He was not given credit for it. Their urban areas were growing, they were putting up apartments and condominiums, and as a result, they thought everything was all right. Their prosperity was blinding them to their true condition.

It is my belief that this same thing has happened to my own country. As a nation, God blinded us with prosperity and with power at the end of World War II, while other nations suffered. We became the big brother to the world. Well, we have been eager to send bombs, but we have not sent what we should have sent: *Bibles.* I am weary of protestations decrying the fact that we used our bombs on other nations but never telling us what we should have sent instead of bombs. My friend, it is the Bible which has made our nation great, and we are pitifully ignorant of it today. The logical, rational conclusion, judging from history, is that God will judge our nation. There is many a great nation lying in rubble and ruin, which reveals God's judgment upon them.

"According to the multitude of his fruit he hath increased the altars." As the population increased, the images increased. In other words, their sin increased as the population increased.

This figure of the vine reminds us of what the Lord Jesus said in John 15 to His Jewish disciples. He said, "I am the true [genuine] vine . . ." (John 15:1, italics mine). He was saying that until then they had felt that their identification with the nation gave them access to God and a relationship to Him. Now this was no longer true. The Lord Jesus was beginning to call out a people to His name. He would be the Head, and the church which He would be forming would be His body. When He said, "I am the genuine vine," He meant that no longer would His people worship through the temple, but they would come through Him to the living God.

> **Their heart is divided; now shall they be found faulty:**
> **he shall break down their altars, he shall spoil their**
> **images [Hos. 10:2].**

"Their heart is divided." Actually they did worship God—we can't say that they didn't. Many of them went down to Jerusalem for the feast days as they had done in former years and joined in the worship of God. However, they would come right back up to the golden calves that had been set up, and they would also worship Baal. Their hearts were divided—one day they would worship God; the next day they would worship Baal.

This is the condition which James mentions in his epistle. "A double-minded man is unstable in all his ways" (James 1:8). I believe this is the reason we find so much inconsistency in the lives of men in public office today. They talk out of one side of their mouths saying one thing; then they talk out of the other side of their mouths saying the opposite thing. I understand that the language of some of our lead-

ers is absolutely the foulest speech one can imagine. Then some of
those same people can appear on television and quote a Bible verse so
that you would think they were sprouting wings under their coats!
That is having a divided heart.

My friend, you cannot go to church on Sunday and sing, "Praise
God from whom all blessings flow," then walk out, and on Monday
morning go to your work and take His name in vain—lose your temper
and use His precious name to damn everything that irritates you. That
kind of divided living is exactly the same kind of divided heart that
brought judgment upon Israel.

> **For now they shall say, We have no king, because we
> feared not the LORD; what then should a king do to us?
> [Hos. 10:3].**

They were saying, "Go down and look at the southern kingdom, and
you will see that their king is not helping them very much." Their
basic problem was not that they had godless kings (they never had one
good king in the northern kingdom), but their own hearts were not
right with God. My friend, it is easy for you and for me to blame our
government for our problems today when the basic problem is in our
own hearts—yours and mine.

> **They have spoken words, swearing falsely in making a
> covenant: thus judgment springeth up as hemlock in the
> furrows of the field [Hos. 10:4].**

The last days of the northern kingdom must have been parallel to our
times. "They have spoken words." They were very loquacious, great
talkers. I believe that in our day radio and television and the printed
page have made our generation the most talkative people on earth.
Man is a pretty talkative "animal"—there is no monkey in a tree that
does more chattering than man does. Talk, talk, talk, talk, reams and
reams of printed material, and about 99.44 percent of all of it is not
worth listening to. It would be better if most of it had never been said.

Yet people are being paid fortunes for what they say and for what they write. Out of it all you hear practically nothing said about bringing people back to God, about a return to God and to the Word of God, about looking to Christ as the Savior.

"They have spoken words, swearing falsely in making a covenant." They just talk, talk, talk, and you can believe almost nothing they say. I hear some Christian people say today that it is terrible that we don't ask people to put their hand on the Bible anymore when they swear to tell the truth in a courtroom. Frankly, I'm glad the Bible is being left out of it. If they are going to lie anyway, all an oath on the Bible would do is blaspheme the Book. If the Bible means nothing to people, why in the world should it be used? I *resent* seeing someone put his hand on the Bible and swear to tell the truth and then hear him lie!

How many Christian people have spoken words to make a false covenant? How many people have marched down to an altar to dedicate their lives to God, have done it repeatedly, and still nothing changed? How often do we say words but not really mean business with God?

"Thus judgment springeth up as hemlock in the furrows of the field." Or, getting it down to the level of most of us, judgment will spring up like weeds in our planted gardens.

The inhabitants of Samaria shall fear because of the calves of Beth-aven: for the people thereof shall mourn over it, and the priests thereof that rejoiced on it, for the glory thereof, because it is departed from it [Hos. 10:5].

"Beth-aven" is a term of ridicule for Bethel. Since one golden calf was located at Bethel and the other at Samaria, the inhabitants of these two cities were jealous of one another over who had the biggest calf or the most gold in it.

"For the people thereof shall mourn over it." The actions of people mourning over these calves is really more the idea of trying to outdo one another over it. It would be in our day like "keeping up with the Joneses." They bought a Cadillac, so we must buy a Continental. They built a house with three bedrooms and three baths, so we must build one with six bedrooms and six baths. They were trying to outdo each other in their calf worship!

"The priests thereof that rejoiced on it, for the glory thereof, because it is departed from it." God is saying, "All the glory of your religion that your priests have boasted in will one day disappear." The word *Ichabod,* meaning "the glory is departed," will be written over the door.

What will happen to it?

It shall be also carried unto Assyria for a present to king Jareb: Ephraim shall receive shame, and Israel shall be ashamed of his own counsel [Hos. 10:6].

Those golden calves are going to be carried into Assyria for a present to the king. They would make a gift fit for a king—after all, there was a lot of gold in those calves.

"Ephraim shall receive shame, and Israel shall be ashamed of his own counsel." Their counsel will come to naught.

As for Samaria, her king is cut off as the foam upon the water [Hos. 10:7].

God makes it very plain that He is going to cut off the king of the northern kingdom. He'll be "cut off as the foam upon the water"—that royal line, as well as the royal line from the southern kingdom, will spend their time singing, "I'm Forever Blowing Bubbles." In other words, they will be reduced to nothing.

The high places also of Aven, the sin of Israel, shall be destroyed: the thorn and the thistle shall come up on their altars; and they shall say to the mountains, Cover us; and to the hills, Fall on us [Hos. 10:8].

"The high places also of Aven . . . shall be destroyed." As we have seen before, they worshiped their idols in groves of trees on the mountains.

"They shall say to the mountains, Cover us; and to the hills, Fall on us." They want to be hidden from the judgment that is coming upon them. This will also be said in the Great Tribulation (see Rev. 6:15–17).

> **O Israel, thou hast sinned from the days of Gibeah: there they stood: the battle in Gibeah against the children of iniquity did not overtake them [Hos. 10:9].**

This probably refers to the terrible events recorded in Judges 19—20. Even after the civil war, and the men of Gibeah were wiped out, the sin remained, and Gibeah was emblematic of gross and cruel sensuality. Along with the idolatrous practices of Israel were also gross sensual sins.

> **It is in my desire that I should chastise them; and the people shall be gathered against them, when they shall bind themselves in their two furrows.**
>
> **And Ephraim is as an heifer that is taught, and loveth to tread out the corn; but I passed over upon her fair neck: I will make Ephraim to ride; Judah shall plow, and Jacob shall break his clods [Hos. 10:10–11].**

"Ephraim is as an heifer that is taught, and loveth to tread out the corn." Ephraim is like an heifer that loves to tread out the corn. They enjoyed the wonderful, bountiful harvest that they got, but they sure didn't like the idea of going out and plowing the ground to break up the clods. God is saying that He will force Ephraim to go back to doing the thing he does not want to do.

> **Sow to yourselves in righteousness, reap in mercy; break up your fallow ground: for it is time to seek the**

LORD, till he come and rain righteousness upon you [Hos. 10:12].

This is a principle that runs throughout the Bible. It is exactly what Paul wrote to the believers in Galatia: "Be not deceived; God is not mocked: for whatsoever a man soweth, that shall he also reap. For he that soweth to his flesh shall of the flesh reap corruption; but he that soweth to the Spirit shall of the Spirit reap life everlasting" (Gal. 6:7–8). Hosea is saying that if they would sow in righteousness, they would reap in mercy. It is always true that we cannot live by the Devil's standards and then expect to reap a reward from God!

Ye have plowed wickedness, ye have reaped iniquity; ye have eaten the fruit of lies: because thou didst trust in thy way, in the multitude of thy mighty men [Hos. 10:13].

Israel hadn't learned her lesson. She plowed wickedness, so she would reap iniquity. They have eaten the fruit of lies. They trusted in mighty men, in their leaders who lied to them. They believed these men rather than God. So they got exactly what was coming to them—the *fruit* of lies.

In Daniel we read that God set over the nation the ". . . basest of men" (Dan. 4:17). My friend, in our day, regardless of what political party you are talking about, a sinful, godless people cannot elect a righteous leader. If the people are liars, they will get a liar as a leader. If they are adulterers, they will get an adulterer. If they are thieves, that's the kind of ruler they will have. My friend, you cannot beat God at this. As the Greek proverb puts it, "The dice of the gods are loaded." You can't gamble with God without losing. If you think that you can be a liar, an adulterer, a thief, and get by with it, I have news for you. When you roll the dice of life, you think they are going to come up in such a way that you will be the winner. Well, God already knows how they will come up, because He has loaded them. When you sow sin, you will reap sin. That is inescapable. If you think that you can escape the results of sin, you are making God out a liar and the Bible a falsehood. It is true that some have thought that they have gotten by with sin, but no one ever has. If we could bring Ahab and Jezebel or Judas back to testify, they would tell you that they did not get by with sin. And if we could bring back to life some Americans who have died, they would testify to the same thing.

Therefore shall a tumult arise among thy people, and all thy fortresses shall be spoiled, as Shalman spoiled Beth-arbel in the day of battle: the mother was dashed in pieces upon her children [Hos. 10:14].

"Shalman" is an abbreviated form of Shalmaneser, the king of Assyria. "Beth-arbel" apparently refers to a place the Greeks call Arbela. It is in the northern part of the country in the region of Galilee. It seems there was a battle here, although it is difficult to identify in secular history just which incident is being referred to in this verse.

"The mother was dashed in pieces upon her children." This was a method used not only by the Assyrians, but also used later on by the Babylonians. This was mentioned by the children of Israel as they wept in Babylon. "O daughter of Babylon, who art to be destroyed; happy shall he be, that rewardeth thee as thou hast served us. Happy shall he be, that taketh and dasheth thy little ones against the stones" (Ps. 137:8–9).

Those people used an awful, brutal, uncivilized method of destruction in war. Was it so uncivilized? Are we any better today? Have you read of things that are done by those in the drug culture, by homosexuals, by demon worshipers, by the new morality of our day? Was dashing the heads of little babies against the stones any worse than the sins that are committed today?

A brokenhearted man in Atlanta, Georgia, said to me one day, "The day I sent my boy to college it would have been better for him if I had taken him to the cemetery and buried him instead." In other words, it would have been better for him to have been brutally killed as a baby by a ruthless pagan. But the ruthless pagans of the present hour are not condemned by our society. Instead they are accepted and even approved.

**So shall Beth-el do unto you because of your great
wickedness: in a morning shall the king of Israel utterly
be cut off [Hos. 10:15].**

The Assyrians came, and overnight Israel was being transported to
Assyria and a life of slavery.

CHAPTERS 11 AND 12

THEME: Israel must be judged, but God will not give her up

Chapter 11 opens on a new note. Up to this point the emphasis has been on the disobedience of God's people, but now there is a new note sounded. That new note is the love of God—how wonderful it is!

When Israel was a child, then I loved him, and called my son out of Egypt [Hos. 11:1].

This verse speaks primarily of the nation Israel—there is no question about that. It reveals the close relationship between God and the nation. In effect God is saying, "Israel as a nation was my son, and I took him out of Egypt. I did not take them out of Egypt because they were wonderful people who were serving Me. They were not serving Me but were in idolatry even then. It was not because of their ability, their superiority; they had nothing like that. I took them out of Egypt because I loved them." My friend, that is the reason He saved you and me. Love is not the basis of salvation, but it is the motive of salvation. Back of the redemption we have in Christ, the fact that He would die, is ". . . God so *loved* the world . . ." (John 3:16, italics mine). "When Israel was a child, then I loved him," God says. "I took him out of Egypt not because he was worthy, not because he performed good works, but because I loved him."

Matthew in his Gospel applied this verse to the Lord Jesus (see Matt. 2:15). This is an example of how statements in the Old Testament can also have application to the future. That baby boy who was born yonder in Bethlehem is identified with these people—He is an Israelite. The woman of Samaria knew this when He came there to the well. She said to him, ". . . How is it that thou, being a Jew, askest drink of me, which am a woman of Samaria? for the Jews have no dealings with the Samaritans" (John 4:9). God sent Him down to this world to die, and the Lord Jesus came and identified Himself with people. As a baby He was taken down to the safety of Egypt, but the time came when God called Him out of the place of safety back to the place of danger within the land. He moved into the arena of life where He was to demonstrate the love of God by dying upon the cross—to furnish a redemption that man might have a righteous basis on which his sins could be forgiven. He identified with His people; He identified with humanity; He identified with you and me. "For God so loved the world, that he gave his only begotten Son, that whosoever believeth in him should not perish, but have everlasting life" (John 3:16).

As they called them, so they went from them: they sacrificed unto Baalim, and burned incense to graven images [Hos. 11:2].

God had put the Canaanites and the other pagans out of the land because they worshiped Baalim. However, when the Hebrews got into the land they also turned to the worship of Baalim and to carved images.

I taught Ephraim also to go, taking them by their arms; but they knew not that I healed them [Hos. 11:3].

God blessed Israel in many different ways, and His blessing was the gentle way in which He led them.

I drew them with cords of a man, with bands of love: and I was to them as they that take off the yoke on their jaws, and I laid meat unto them [Hos. 11:4].

God says, "I did not force them to serve Me." God will not force Himself upon you either, my friend. Many people say, "Why doesn't God break through today? Why doesn't He do this or that?" I don't know why God doesn't do a lot of things—He just hasn't told me. He is God, and I happen to be a little creature down here and I lack a great deal of information. Although I'm not able to answer that, I do know this: God will not force you. The only band He will put on you is the band of love. He says, "I won't bridle you, I won't push you, the only appeal I make to you is that I love you." My friend, that is the appeal that God makes to you and to me today. He moved heaven and hell to get to the door of your heart, but He stopped there and politely knocks on the door and says, "Behold, I stand at the door, and knock . . ." (Rev. 3:20). That is where He is—He has never crashed the door; He is not going to push Himself in. You will have to respond to His love.

It is interesting that love has always been the strongest appeal. It is said that Napoleon made the statement, "Charlemagne, Alexander the Great, and other generals have built up empires, and they built them on force, but Jesus Christ today has millions of people who would die for Him, and He built an empire on love." That is His only appeal to you—don't think He will use any other method. He will judge you, but He will not draw you to Himself except by love. That is the strongest appeal that can possible be made. The band is a band of love.

> **He shall not return into the land of Egypt, but the Assyrian shall be his king, because they refused to return [Hos. 11:5].**

Israel ran down to Egypt to get help but then found out that Egypt was his enemy. Then he ran up to Assyria to get help there. God said, "I'm going to make Assyria his king"—Assyria is where He sent Israel into captivity.

> **And the sword shall abide on his cities, and shall consume his branches, and devour them, because of their own counsels.**

> **And my people are bent to backsliding from me: though they called them to the most High, none at all would exalt him [Hos. 11:6–7].**

This is the second time in Hosea that the word *backsliding* occurs. Again, it is the figure of the backsliding heifer, that little calf who, when you try to push her up the runway into the old wagon, simply puts down her front feet and begins to slide backwards—and you just have to start all over again. That is a picture of what backsliding is—it is to refuse to listen to God, to refuse to come to Him.

> **How shall I give thee up, Ephraim? how shall I deliver thee, Israel? how shall I make thee as Admah? how shall I set thee as Zeboim? mine heart is turned within me, my repentings are kindled together.**
>
> **I will not execute the fierceness of mine anger, I will not return to destroy Ephraim: for I am God, and not man; the Holy One in the midst of thee: and I will not enter into the city [Hos. 11:8–9].**

This is a plaintive note. It seems as if God is on the horns of a dilemma here, as if He is frustrated. Listen to Him: "How shall I give thee up, Ephraim?" He doesn't want to give them up. God loves them, but because of their sin God must judge them.

"How shall I deliver thee, Israel?" My friend, God has no other way to save you except by the death of Christ. You may think you have two or three different ways yourself, but God has but one way. Since He says, "There is no saviour beside me" (Hos. 13:4), you had better listen to Him. You and I are not in the saving business, but He is.

"How shall I make thee as Admah? how shall I set thee as Zeboim?" Admah and Zeboim were cities down on the plain which God judged along with Sodom and Gomorrah. God is saying to Israel, "I hate to judge you like that." However, God had to judge them, and today it is just as desolate in Samaria as it is there along the Dead Sea where these cities were once located.

"Mine heart is turned within me, my repentings are kindled together. I will not execute the fierceness of mine anger." In other words, Israel did not receive half of what they deserved. Why? Because God says, "I will not return to destroy Ephraim"—He intends to redeem them and to put these people back in that land some day. Their present return to the land is not a fulfillment of this at all; do not blame God for what is happening in that land today.

However, God *will* put them back in the land. Why will He do it? For one reason: "For I am God, and not man; the Holy One in the midst of thee: and I will not enter into the city." This is something else we need to learn today. We feel like we live in a democracy and that our government exists for us and exists to carry out the decisions we make, but God says, "I am the sovereign God. I'm not accountable to anyone. I do not have a board of directors, and nobody elected Me to office. I do what I please." My friend, if you do not like what God is doing today, it's too bad for you, because God is going to do it—He is not accountable to you. There are a lot of things which God does that I don't understand, but He is God, and He is surely not accountable to Vernon McGee. He does not come down and hand in a report to me. The folk who work for me at "Thru the Bible" headquarters hand in reports to me, but God doesn't give me a report. Why? Because He is *God*, and He doesn't have to report to me.

> **They shall walk after the LORD: he shall roar like a lion: when he shall roar, then the children shall tremble from the west [Hos. 11:10].**

God intends to judge, my friend—a judgment upon the nations in the west. And the United States happens to be *west* from the land of Israel.

> **They shall tremble as a bird out of Egypt, and as a dove out of the land of Assyria: and I will place them in their houses, saith the LORD.**

> **Ephraim compasseth me about with lies, and the house of Israel with deceit: but Judah yet ruleth with God, and is faithful with the saints [Hos. 11:11–12].**

Judah still had a few good kings in the southern kingdom, but there were none in the northern kingdom. Some of the kings made a profession, but they were using lies and deceit. My friend, I believe we live in a day when you can fool everyone. Abraham Lincoln made the statement (everybody believes it because good old Abe said it), "You can fool some of the people all of the time, and all of the people some of the time, but you cannot fool all of the people all of the time." Lincoln did not live in this day of television and brainwashing. You can fool all the people all the time. There has never been such a day of brainwashing as today. But nobody is fooling God. He knows, and someday He will judge according to truth.

Chapter 12 continues God's statement of judgment against Israel.

> **Ephraim feedeth on wind, and followeth after the east wind: he daily increaseth lies and desolation; and they do make a covenant with the Assyrians, and oil is carried into Egypt [Hos. 12:1].**

"Ephraim feedeth on wind, and followeth after the east wind." This is a reference to the east wind which comes over the burning Arabian desert and blows through that land. God is saying, "I intend to let the Assyrians come through the land just like the east wind."

> **The LORD hath also a controversy with Judah, and will punish Jacob according to his ways; according to his doings will he recompense him.**
>
> **He took his brother by the heel in the womb, and by his strength he had power with God:**
>
> **Yea, he had power over the angel, and prevailed: he wept, and made supplication unto him: he found him in Beth-el, and there he spake with us [Hos. 12:2–4].**

Many people have questioned why God put it in His Word that Jacob took hold of his brother Esau's heel. It is interesting to note that today medicine and psychology have said that probably the most important period of a man's life is when he is in the womb, because even in the womb character is being formed as well as the human body. This little fellow Jacob began to reveal something in the womb—he revealed that he wanted to be the firstborn. Although Esau beat him out, Jacob wanted to be the firstborn. I do not know how to explain it other than to say that it was in his heart from the very beginning. He wrestled at his birth, and God had to wrestle with him later on in his life at Peniel to bring him to submission so that He would be able to bless him. "Yea, he had power over the angel, and prevailed." How did he prevail? Was he a better wrestler? Would he appear on television today as an outstanding wrestler? No, Jacob wasn't much of a wrestler. He had his ears pinned back and his shoulders pinned to the mat. God had him down, but he won. How did he win? By surrendering. My friend, you can fight God all you want to, but you'll never win until you surrender to Him.

Even the LORD God of hosts; the LORD is his memorial [Hos. 12:5].

The name *Jehovah*, or "the LORD," is a name God gave to Israel as a memorial. He said, "You will always know Me by My name. I am Jehovah, the self-existing one, the living God." We do not need images to remind us of God. His very name expresses His nature.

Therefore turn thou to thy God: keep mercy and judgment, and wait on thy God continually [Hos. 12:6].

These people needed to practice what they preached. In our day, the worship of Satan and the giving over to homosexuality is leading to the basest of crimes. Only by coming to the living God and waiting upon Him continually will we have mercy and justice; they go together—you will not have one without the other.

He is a merchant, the balances of deceit are in his hand: he loveth to oppress [Hos. 12:7].

This speaks of dishonesty in business, something of which God does not approve.

> And Ephraim said, Yet I am become rich, I have found
> me out substance: in all my labours, they shall find
> none iniquity in me that were sin [Hos. 12:8].

In other words, Ephraim felt he was able to buy his way with money. He had made his money dishonestly, but he thought he was being blessed of God.

> And I that am the LORD thy God from the land of Egypt
> will yet make thee to dwell in tabernacles, as in the days
> of the solemn feast [Hos. 12:9].

God is saying to Israel, "I am not through with you—I'll not give you up."

> Is there iniquity in Gilead? surely they are vanity: they
> sacrifice bullocks in Gilgal; yea, their altars are as
> heaps in the furrows of the fields [Hos. 12:11].

"Is there iniquity in Gilead?" Gilead is the place where there should be a balm to heal the wound, but Gilead was then a place of sin.

> Ephraim provoked him to anger most bitterly: therefore
> shall he leave his blood upon him, and his reproach
> shall his Lord return unto him [Hos. 12:14].

"Therefore shall he leave his blood upon him." His blood shall rest upon his own head, for he is guilty and deserves death. Blood had been shed profusely, and the guilt of his sin remained upon him.

Israel had turned from God, and therefore He must judge them.

CHAPTERS 13 AND 14

THEME: Israel will be judged in the present; Israel will be saved in the future

ISRAEL WILL BE JUDGED IN THE PRESENT

In chapter 13 we see that God's judgment of Israel is inevitable.

When Ephraim spake trembling, he exalted himself in Israel; but when he offended in Baal, he died [Hos. 13:1].

In other words, when Ephraim served the living God, God exalted him; but when he began the worship of Baal, he died. My friend, not only did Ephraim die and was put out of the land, but the land also died, and I do not think that it has come back today. The ruins of Samaria and the other cities in that area are the most desolate that you will find anywhere on the earth.

And now they sin more and more, and have made them molten images of their silver, and idols according to their own understanding, all of it the work of the craftsmen: they say of them, Let the men that sacrifice kiss the calves [Hos. 13:2].

This was a form of worship. The people were actually going up and kissing those golden calves!

There are many people today who think that to kiss a certain image or to kiss a certain area of ground is to worship God. On one of our tours to Israel there was a lady who got down on her hands and knees at the Garden Tomb and started kissing the place. I immediately took her by the arm and reminded her that we had been told not even to drink the water in that land and that she must get up out of the dirt.

"Oh," she said, "that doesn't make any difference. This is a holy place; this is where my Lord was buried." Then I said to her, "He's not here today. He is the living Christ at God's right hand. You cannot kiss Him today, but you can worship Him and praise Him." It is nonsense to go around kissing something as an act of worship of the living and true God. You worship Him, my friend, by the life that you live. You worship Him in the way you conduct your business, carry on your social life, the way you run your home, and the way you act out on the street—not only in the way you act in the sanctuary. We are the ones who have made a distinction between the sanctuary and the street, but in God's sight there is no difference at all.

> **Therefore they shall be as the morning cloud, and as the early dew that passeth away, as the chaff that is driven with the whirlwind out of the floor, and as the smoke out of the chimney.**

> **Yet I am the LORD thy God from the land of Egypt, and thou shalt know no god but me: for there is no saviour beside me [Hos. 13:3–4].**

Listen to Him, my friend. You may work out a plan of salvation, but He is the only Savior, and since He is, you had better come His way. The Lord Jesus said, ". . . I am the way, the truth, and the life: no man cometh unto the Father, but by me" (John 14:6). Now either that's true or it's not true. Millions of people have come that way, and they have found it to be true. You may think you have your way of salvation, but God is the only Savior, and He is the only one who can offer you a plan of salvation.

> **I did know thee in the wilderness, in the land of great drought.**

> **According to their pasture, so were they filled; they were filled, and their heart was exalted; therefore have they forgotten me [Hos. 13:5–6].**

God says, "I have been your God, the one who brought you out of Egypt. I am not about to give you up, but I am going to judge you."

Therefore I will be unto them as a lion: as a leopard by the way will I observe them:

I will meet them as a bear that is bereaved of her whelps, and will rend the caul of their heart, and there will I devour them like a lion: the wild beast shall tear them [Hos. 13:7–8].

There is a prophetic sidelight here that is very interesting. In Daniel's vision (ch. 7) Babylon is pictured as a lion, Greece (under Alexander the Great) is pictured as a leopard, and the empire of Media-Persia is pictured as the bear. Now here in Hosea's prophecy God is saying that in the future He will come against them like a lion and a leopard, but in the *immediate* future He will come like a bear—represented by Media-Persia, which at that early date was dominated by Assyria. God says, "I will meet them as a bear that is bereaved of her whelps." There is nothing more ferocious than a mother bear that has been robbed of her cubs, and she is an apt illustration of the brutal Assyrian army.

O Israel, thou hast destroyed thyself; but in me is thine help [Hos. 13:9].

We often blame God for what happens to us. When you feel like that, this is a good verse to turn to. *You* have destroyed *yourself*, and you are responsible for your condition. But you can get help from God; *He* will furnish help to you.

I will be thy king: where is any other that may save thee in all thy cities? and thy judges of whom thou saidst, Give me a king and princes?

I gave thee a king in mine anger, and took him away in my wrath [Hos. 13:10–11].

"I gave thee a king in mine anger." When Israel asked for a king, God gave Saul to them. "And took him away in my wrath." He took the last king, Hoshea, away from the northern kingdom, He took Zedekiah away from the southern kingdom, and He did it in His wrath. Judgment! It was His judgment in the beginning, and His judgment at the end.

Samaria shall become desolate; for she hath rebelled against her God: they shall fall by the sword: their infants shall be dashed in pieces, and their women with child shall be ripped up [Hos. 13:16].

"Samaria shall become desolate." I have been to Samaria, and I agree with God. It is a desolate place today.

ISRAEL WILL BE SAVED IN THE FUTURE

Chapter 14 is a wonderful chapter, for it speaks of the future salvation of Israel.

O Israel, return unto the LORD thy God; for thou hast fallen by thine iniquity [Hos. 14:1].

The Lord tells the people that it is because of their sin that they will go into captivity.

Asshur shall not save us; we will not ride upon horses: neither will we say any more to the work of our hands, Ye are our gods: for in thee the fatherless findeth mercy [Hos. 14:3].

Imagine making something with your hands and then falling down and worshiping it! Many men today worship their own ability. They worship their brain, their intellect. They worship what they are doing and what they are able to do. You are nothing but a pagan and a heathen when you do that, my friend.

> I will heal their backsliding, I will love them freely: for
> mine anger is turned away from him.
>
> I will be as the dew unto Israel: he shall grow as the lily,
> and cast forth his roots as Lebanon.
>
> His branches shall spread, and his beauty shall be as
> the olive tree, and his smell as Lebanon.
>
> They that dwell under his shadow shall return; they
> shall revive as the corn, and grow as the vine: the scent
> thereof shall be as the wine of Lebanon [Hos. 14:4–7].

"I will hear their backsliding." God says, "The people have been back-sliding, slipping away from Me, but I am going to heal them. I will love them freely, for Mine anger is turned away from them."

> Ephraim shall say, What have I to do any more with
> idols? I have heard him, and observed him: I am like a
> green fir tree. From me is thy fruit found.
>
> Who is wise, and he shall understand these things? pru-
> dent, and he shall know them? for the ways of the LORD
> are right, and the just shall walk in them: but the trans-
> gressors shall fall therein [Hos. 14:8–9].

Verse 8 is one of the most wonderful verses in the Bible. This is a victory song. "Ephraim *shall* say"—this is future. God is finally going to win. Love is going to win the victory here. God has said to Ephraim, "Oh, Ephraim, how shall I give you up?" And He said, "Ephraim—let him alone because he has turned to idols." Now God says, "But there is a day coming when Ephraim will see that he's made a great blunder and mistake, and he will turn back to Me. He is going to say, 'I don't have anything more to do with idols.'"

I cannot help but believe in the midst of this tragedy of sin, this drama of human life which is being enacted down here in this world today, that God is going to come out the victor. I believe that there are going to be more people saved than there will be lost. That was Spurgeon's belief also; he said that many times. You and I have our noses pressed against the present hour. We look around at the world today, and all we see is the little flock the Lord Jesus talked about—that is, the church, the people whom He is calling out of this world. But there are many whom He has saved in the past. For example, at one time He saved the entire population of Nineveh (although a hundred years later they reverted to sin, and He judged them). There have been other great revival movements in the past also, but the greatest turning to God is to take place in the future. That will occur, of all times, during the Great Tribulation period. The Millennium is also going to be a period of salvation, by the way. God is going to win, my friend. Love will triumph. Our God today is riding victoriously in His own chariot—He is the sovereign God. God pity the man who gets under those chariot wheels! I don't know about you, but I want to go along with God—I'm hitchhiking a ride with Him today. That is the reason it is so urgent that we know His Word—to find out how to stay in His will in this difficult day in which we are living.

BIBLIOGRAPHY

(Recommended for Further Study)

Feinberg, Charles L. *The Minor Prophets*. Chicago, Illinois: Moody Press, 1976.

Gaebelein, Arno C. *The Annotated Bible*. 1917. Reprint. Neptune, New Jersey: Loizeaux Brothers, 1971.

Ironside, H. A. *The Minor Prophets*. Neptune, New Jersey: Loizeaux Brothers, n.d.

Jensen, Irving L. *Minor Prophets of Israel*. Chicago, Illinois: Moody Press, 1975.

Unger, Merrill F. *Unger's Commentary on the Old Testament*, Vol. 2. Chicago, Illinois: Moody Press, 1982.

JOEL

The Book of
JOEL

INTRODUCTION

The prophecy of Joel may seem unimportant as it contains only three brief chapters. However, this little book is like an atom bomb—it is not very big, but it sure is potent and powerful.

We know very little about the prophet Joel. All we are told concerning him is in Joel 1:1, "The word of the LORD that came to Joel the son of Pethuel." *Joel* means "Jehovah is God," and it was a very common name. There have been some people who have jumped to the conclusion that the prophet Joel was a son of Samuel because 1 Samuel 8:1–2 says, "And it came to pass, when Samuel was old, that he made his sons judges over Israel. Now the name of his firstborn was Joel . . ." But if we read further the next verse tells us, "And his sons walked not in his ways, but turned aside after lucre, and took bribes, and perverted judgment" (1 Sam. 8:3). Samuel's son could not have been the same as the prophet Joel.

We can be sure that Joel prophesied in Jerusalem and the Jerusalem area. Throughout his prophecy he refers again and again to "the house of the LORD." For instance, in Joel 1:9 we read, "The meat offering and the drink offering is cut off from the house of the LORD; the priests, the LORD's ministers, mourn." He also mentions Jerusalem in Joel 3:20, "But Judah shall dwell for ever, and Jerusalem from generation to generation." And then again, in Joel 3:17, we read, "So shall ye know that I am the LORD your God dwelling in Zion, my holy mountain: then shall Jerusalem be holy, and there shall no strangers pass through her any more." Therefore we know that this man was a prophet in the southern kingdom of Judah.

Joel prophesied as one of the early prophets. Actually there were quite a few prophets—at least fifty—and it is generally conceded by conservative scholars that Joel prophesied about the time of the reign of Joash, king of Judah. That would mean that he was contemporary with and probably knew Elijah and Elisha.

Joel's theme is "the day of the LORD." He makes specific reference to it five times: Joel 1:15; 2:1–2; 2:10–11; 2:30–31; and 3:14–16. Isaiah, Jeremiah, Ezekiel, and Daniel all refer to the Day of the Lord. Sometimes they call it "that day." Zechariah particularly emphasizes "that day." What is "that day"? It is the Day of the Lord, or the Day of Jehovah. Joel is the one who introduces the Day of the Lord in prophecy. Yonder from the mountaintop of the beginning of written prophecy, this man looked down through the centuries, seeing further than any other prophet saw—he saw the Day of the Lord.

The Day of the Lord is a technical expression in Scripture which is fraught with meaning. It includes the millennial Kingdom which will come at the second coming of Christ, but Joel is going to make it very clear to us that it begins with the Great Tribulation period, the time of great trouble. If you want to set a boundary or parenthesis at the end of the Day of the Lord, it would be the end of the Millennium when the Lord Jesus puts down all unrighteousness and establishes His eternal Kingdom here upon the earth.

The Day of the Lord is also an expression that is peculiar to the prophets of the Old Testament. It does not include the period when the church is in the world, because none of the prophets spoke about a group of people who would be called out from among the Gentiles, the nation Israel, and all the tribes of the earth, to be brought into one great body called the church which would be raptured out of this world. The prophets neither spoke nor wrote about the church.

James, at the great council of Jerusalem, more or less outlined the relationship between the church age and this period known as the Day of the Lord. He said, "Simeon hath declared how God at the first did visit the Gentiles, to take out of them a people for his name. And to this agree the words of the prophets; as it is written, After this I will return, and will build again the tabernacle of David, which is fallen down; and I will build again the ruins thereof, and I will set it up"

(Acts 15:14–16). James says, "After this"—after what? *After* He calls out the church from this world, God will again turn to His program with Israel, and it is to this time that the Day of the Lord refers. James went on to say, "That the residue of men might seek after the Lord, and all the Gentiles, upon whom my name is called, saith the Lord, who doeth all these things" (Acts 15:17). Today God is calling *out* of the Gentiles a people; in that day, *all* the Gentiles who will be entering the Kingdom will seek the Lord. I think there will be a tremendous turning to God at that time unlike any the church has ever witnessed.

Someone may question, "Why is God following this program?" James said, "Known unto God are all his works from the beginning of the world" (Acts 15:18). Don't ask me why God is following this program—ask Him, because I do not know and nobody else knows. He is following this program because it is *His* program and it is *His* universe. He is not responsible to you or to me. God doesn't turn in a report at the end of the week to tell us what He's been doing and to receive our approval. My friend, all I can say is that it is just too bad if you and I don't like it because, after all, we are just creatures down here in this world.

There are several special features about the prophecy of Joel which I would like to point out. Joel was the first of the writing prophets, and as he looked down through the centuries, he saw the coming of the Day of the Lord. However, I do not think he saw the church at all—none of the prophets did. When the Lord Jesus went to the top of the Mount of Olives, men who were schooled in the Old Testament came and asked Him, "What is the sign of the end of the age?" Our Lord didn't mention His Cross to them at that time. He didn't tell them then about the coming of the Holy Spirit. He didn't tell them about the church period or mention the Rapture to them. Instead, the Lord went way down to the beginning of the Day of the Lord. He dated it, but it's not on your calendar or mine; the events He predicted will identify it for the people who will be there when the Day of the Lord begins: "When ye therefore shall see the abomination of desolation, spoken of by Daniel the prophet, stand in the holy place, (whoso readeth, let him understand:)" (Matt. 24:15). That is how we are to know the beginning of the Day of the Lord. Joel will make it clear to us that it begins with night—that is, it begins as a time of trouble. After all, the Hebrew day always began at sunset. Genesis tells us, "And the evening and the morning were the first day" (Gen. 1:5). We begin at sunup, but God begins at sundown. The Day of the Lord, therefore, begins with night.

It is remarkable to note that, unlike Hosea, Joel says practically nothing about himself. In Hosea we find out about the scandal that went on in his home, about his unfaithful wife. We do not know whether Joel had an unfaithful wife or not; we don't even know if he was married. The very first verse of the prophecy gives us all that we are to know: "The word of the LORD that came to Joel the son of Pethuel" (Joel 1:1).

Unlike many of the other prophets, Joel does not condemn Israel for idolatry. Earlier in their history, at the time Joel was prophesying, idolatry was not the great sin in Israel. Joel will only mention one sin, the sin of drunkenness.

Joel opens his prophecy with a unique description of a literal plague of locusts. Then he uses that plague of locusts to compare with the future judgments which will come upon this earth. The first chapter is a dramatic and literary gem. It is a remarkable passage of Scripture, unlike anything you will find elsewhere in literature.

Finally, Joel's prophecy contains the very controversial passage in which he mentions the outpouring of the Holy Spirit which was referred to by the apostle Peter on the Day of Pentecost (see Joel 2:28–29). There is a difference of interpretation concerning the pouring out of the Holy Spirit, and we will look at that in detail when we come to it.

OUTLINE

I. **Literal and Local Plague of Locusts, Chapter 1:1–14**

II. **Looking to the Day of the Lord (Prelude), Chapters 1:15—2:32**

III. **Looking at the Day of the Lord (Postlude), Chapter 3**
   A. The Great Tribulation, Chapter 3:1–15
   B. The Millennial Kingdom, Chapter 3:16–21

CHAPTER 1

THEME: Literal and local plague of locusts; looking to the Day of the Lord (prelude)

The prophecy of Joel contains only three very brief chapters, but it holds an important position in Scripture. As the first of the writing prophets, it is Joel who introduces and defines the term, "the day of the LORD."

LITERAL AND LOCAL PLAGUE OF LOCUSTS

The word of the LORD that came to Joel the son of Pethuel [Joel 1:1].

There are those who have thought that Joel was a son of Samuel (see 1 Sam. 8:1–2), but Samuel's sons were very wicked and this Joel certainly is not. This boy's father was Pethuel. Joel was a common name, and it means "Jehovah is God."

Hear this, ye old men, and give ear, all ye inhabitants of the land. Hath this been in your days, or even in the days of your fathers? [Joel 1:2].

Apparently Israel was in the midst of a great locust plague at this time. Locust plagues were rather commonplace in that land, but Joel calls to the old men and says, "Did anything like this ever happen in your day? Did it happen in the day of your fathers? Have you ever heard anything like this locust plague?" Of course, they had to say, "No, this is the worst we've ever had." The trouble with most of us as we begin to get older is that we have grandiose ideas about the past. If some young person comes and says to us, "Say, we just had a wonderful meeting at our church," we like to say, "That's wonderful, that was a great meeting, but we had a meeting that was twice as good back in my hometown when I was young." Joel said, "You old men have never heard of anything like this"—and the old men had to agree that they had not.

Tell ye your children of it, and let your children tell their children, and their children another generation [Joel 1:3].

Joel goes on to say, "You can pass this on down. Tell your children about this and have them tell their children, because there's not going to be a plague of locusts like this ever again." Does this remind you of another passage of Scripture? In the Olivet Discourse in Matthew 24, when the Lord Jesus identified the period which He Himself labeled the Great Tribulation period, He said the same thing about it. He said that there has never been anything like it before, and there is not going to be anything like it afterward. Now that more or less puts parentheses around that period and slips it into a unique slot in history. During the Great Tribulation no one will be able to say, "This reminds me of when I was a young fellow—we had a real time of trouble back then." We have never had a period like the Great Tribulation. For all periods of recorded history in the past, there have always been previous times in history that could match it. However, the Lord Jesus made it very clear concerning the Great Tribulation: "For then shall be great tribulation, such as was not since the beginning of the world to this time, no, nor ever shall be" [Matt. 24:21]. When people are in the midst of the Great Tribulation, there will be none of this questioning that we hear today: "Do you think that the Great Depression was the Great Tribulation?" Or, "Do you think that all this turmoil today is the Great Tribulation?" The answer is very easy to come by when we turn to the words of the Lord Jesus. He said there is nothing like it in the past. We've had times like this before, my friend—they can all be duplicated in the past. And since things are not getting better but getting worse, neither can we say there will be nothing like this in the future.

In a very dramatic way, Joel is saying, "Look, this locust plague is unique—there has never been anything like it, but there is coming another unique period called the Day of the Lord." The Day of the Lord will open with the Great Tribulation after the church has left this world. It will be a frightful time on this earth, horrible beyond description, and then Christ will come and establish His Kingdom. I wish the people who deny that the Bible teaches these things would study the total Word of God and not just lift out a few verses here and there. We need to study the *entire* Word of God to know what it says.

This plague of locusts stands alone as being different from any other plague that has taken place. The plague of locusts in the land of Egypt at the time of Moses was a miraculous plague—it was a judgment of God. However, this plague was what we would call a natural event.

There are several things that we need to understand about the locust as many of us are not familiar with them at all. As a boy I always enjoyed lying on my bed before an open window on a summer evening and listening to the locusts in the trees. However, they were never a plague, and they probably were not the same kind of locusts which were in Israel in Bible times or even today. If you have ever seen pictures of fields after a plague of locusts, you know that locusts seem to have a scorched earth policy of their own—it looks just as if a fire had burned over the field and destroyed everything.

The Word of God speaks of locusts, and one passage I will draw your attention to is Proverbs 30:27, "The locusts have no king, yet go they forth all of them by bands." Locusts march as an army, and they are divided into different bands as they go. That will help us understand Joel's description of this locust plague as we come to verse 4—

That which the palmerworm hath left hath the locust eaten; and that which the locust hath left hath the cankerworm eaten; and that which the cankerworm hath left hath the caterpillar eaten [Joel 1:4].

It is true that four different words are used here—the palmerworm, the locust, the cankerworm, and the caterpillar. There are those who believe that this refers to four different types of insects, but there really is no basis for that. The *palmerworm* means "to gnaw off." The word for *locust* in Hebrew is *arbeh* and it suggests that there are many of them and they are migratory—they move as a great swarm. The *cank-erworm* means "to lick off," and the *caterpillar* means "to devour or to consume." These four words describe the locust and what he does. The locusts move in bands just like an army. First of all, there are the planes which come over and drop the bombs. Then after the bombs have been dropped by the air corps, the artillery comes through and destroys every section, leaving great areas devastated, but a great deal remains. Then the infantry comes along—that's the third group—and they get what has been left. The mop-up crew follows after that, and they will get what little may still be there. What we have here, there-fore, are four words which describe the different bands of locusts. They have no general, they have no king, they have no lieutenants or sergeants, but they move just like an army.

Locusts were often sent by God as a judgment, but we would put this plague in the category of a natural plague. I believe that it was not necessarily a judgment, but a warning to the people, a warning to the nation. Joel was the first writing prophet, and he prophesied at the same time as Elijah. As Elijah was warning the northern kingdom, this man Joel, in a most dramatic manner, was warning the southern kingdom of a judgment that was coming. He will move from the local judgment—it was the method of all the prophets to move from the local situation into the future—to the judgment that is coming at the Day of the Lord.

The Day of the Lord is one of the most misunderstood terms and yet one of the most important in Scripture. Joel was the first to use it, and he makes very clear what the Day of the Lord is. After him, all the other prophets had to do was to speak of "that day," and it was under-stood as to what they were referring.

Now I am getting a little bit ahead of this chapter, but I want to say that Joel will move from this literal and local plague of locusts to speak of the Day of the Lord which begins with the Great Tribulation period. How does the Great Tribulation period open? It opens with the four horsemen of the Apocalypse: there is a false peace, then war breaks out, followed by a famine, and then finally the pale horse of death. I see a tremendous parallel between these four bands of locusts and the four horsemen of the Apocalypse. During the Great Tribulation period it will not be literal locusts, but it will be something far worse that is going to ride, not just through that land, but through the entire world. The world will be totally devastated when the Lord Jesus Christ returns to the earth to set up His Kingdom.

Awake, ye drunkards, and weep; and howl, all ye drinkers of wine, because of the new wine, for it is cut off from your mouth [Joel 1:5].

The locusts have gotten to the grapes first. They have stripped all the vineyards, and there will be no more wine for the drunkards. The man who was an alcoholic in that day found himself taking the cure before he intended to because there was no more wine to drink.

This reveals that, even at the beginning of the downfall of the nation Israel, the great sin was drunkenness. We are frequently reminded that most of the accidents which take place on our highways are caused by some individual who is exercising his freedom and right to drink. Entire families have been killed on the highway while out on a holiday because some drunk driver has hit them head-on. I may be criticized for moving into the realm of politics, but, my friend, I am studying the Word of God, and when it talks about drunkenness, I am going to talk about drunkenness. And when God's Word speaks about the king being a drunkard, then I will talk about drunkenness in my nation's capital. When we are told that there are dozens of cocktail parties every day in Washington, D.C., it is no wonder that some of the decisions which are being handed down look as if they were coming from men who are not in their right minds.

"Awake, ye drunkards, and weep; and howl, all ye drinkers of wine." At the very beginning, drunkenness was beginning to chip away the foundation of the nation Israel. This is the only sin Joel will mention. He will not mention idolatry at all, the great sin of turning from God, which eventually brought the nation down. At this time the people still made a profession of worshiping God.

For a nation is come up upon my land, strong, and without number, whose teeth are the teeth of a lion, and he hath the cheek teeth of a great lion [Joel 1:6].

Here the locusts are compared to an invading army and its destructiveness. These little bitty insects, the locusts, can tear a tree down. They can move through a field of grain and absolutely leave nothing but bare ground. They came along in these four bands with no leader, no king. They came, in most cases, as a judgment from God, but this plague was a warning from God. Later Joel will move ahead to that which is still future, the Day of the Lord which will be just like a locust plague upon the earth. The four horsemen of the Apocalypse are yet to ride.

> **He hath laid my vine waste, and barked my fig tree: he hath made it clean bare, and cast it away; the branches thereof are made white [Joel 1:7].**

The locusts actually can kill a fig tree. They absolutely stripped a fig tree of its bark, leaving nothing but the naked wood exposed.

Joel is sending out a message to the people, and he is going to tell them what they are to do at a time like this. He will tell them ten things they are to do—

> **Lament like a virgin girded with sackcloth for the husband of her youth [Joel 1:8].**

He says something now that is unusual: (1) They are to *lament*. Like a young bride who has lost her husband, perhaps killed in battle, that is the way this nation should weep.

> **The meat offering and the drink offering is cut off from the house of the LORD; the priests, the LORD's ministers, mourn [Joel 1:9].**

"The meat offering and the drink offering is cut off from the house of the LORD." In other words, they are not able to make an offering at all. (2) "The priests, the LORD's ministers, *mourn*." All through this passage the same thing is said. The drunkards mourned and the priests mourned—the entire economy was affected by this plague.

This verse and other verses lead us to believe that the prophet Joel was in Jerusalem. He speaks here to the priests who minister in the house of the Lord.

The field is wasted, the land mourneth; for the corn is wasted: the new wine is dried up, the oil languisheth [Joel 1:10].

There was no olive oil and no grapes and no grain. The three staple crops which they had were now destroyed. Even the land is to mourn. You see, the land and the people were closely intertwined. The Mosaic Law was not only given to a people, it was given to a land.

Joel has spoken to the drunkards, he has spoken to the priests, and now he will speak to the farmers:

Be ye ashamed, O ye husbandmen; howl, O ye vine-dressers, for the wheat and for the barley; because the harvest of the field is perished.

The vine is dried up, and the fig tree languisheth; the pomegranate tree, the palm tree also, and the apple tree, even all the trees of the field, are withered: because joy is withered away from the sons of men [Joel 1:11–12].

(3) "*Be ye ashamed,* O ye husbandmen." (4) "*Howl,* O ye vinedressers." The vinedressers are vineyard owners. "The apple tree" is actually the orange tree which is indigenous to that land.

Gird yourselves, and lament, ye priests: howl, ye ministers of the altar: come, lie all night in sackcloth, ye ministers of my God: for the meat offering and the drink offering is withholden from the house of your God [Joel 1:13].

(5) "*Gird yourselves,*" (6) "*and lament,* ye priests: howl, ye ministers of the altar." The priests could not perform their function because there was nothing for them to use for the offerings. They were to lie all

night girded with sackcloth and ashes because there was no meat offering and no drink offering. The economy of the land was wrecked,
and there was not even enough to make an offering to God. However,
God makes it clear that it was not the ritual that was important but the
hearts of the people.

In these verses God is asking the people to do something that He
had not asked before. When God gave the Mosaic Law, He gave seven
feast days to these people, and He made it clear that He did not want
them to come before Him with a long face. He wanted them to come to
His house rejoicing and with joy in their hearts.

Have you noticed today that when Christians meet together in
church it is generally not a very joyful occasion? I am even rebuked for
telling funny stories. Sometimes I see a lot of saints who just sit there
and do not even crack a smile. I wish they would—I think it would do
them good. There is no joy today, and there was no joy in Joel's day.

Why is God for the first time telling His people, "I want you to
lament. I want you in sackcloth and ashes. I want you to mourn"?
Before He had told them, "I want you to come before Me with joy." The
reason is because of sin in the nation. That is the same reason there is
such a lack of joy today. The world is surely working hard today. The
music has to be loud and fast, and the jokes have to be dirty to even get
a laugh. Even in our churches it is considered almost sinful to laugh
out loud. Oh, my friend, where is our joy today? It is gone because of
sin. God won't let us have joy. He said to these people, "Come before
Me now with your mourning. I do not like it, but you are sinful and I
want to see your repentance."

**Sanctify ye a fast, call a solemn assembly, gather the
elders and all the inhabitants of the land into the house
of the LORD your God, and cry unto the LORD [Joel 1:14].**

(7) *"Sanctify ye a fast."* God had never asked them to do that before.
God had given them feast days—He never gave them a fast day until
they plunged into sin. The one sin Joel mentions which was destroy-
ing the nation was drunkenness. It was robbing people of their normal
thinking; they were not able to make right judgments.

(8) *"Call a solemn assembly."* In other words, they were to come together. God had wanted them to come together and rejoice in His presence, but now He says this is to be a solemn assembly.

(9) *"Gather the elders and all the inhabitants of the land into the house of the* LORD *your God."* This was a time to go to church. During World War II there were two rather godless men who were good friends and belonged to all different kinds of clubs (drinking clubs, most of them), but they met one Sunday at church. One of them said, "Well, I didn't know you went to church!" The other replied, "I don't usually go to church—this is my first time. But I've got a son over there fighting in this war, and I thought it was about time I got to church." My friend, times of great trouble drive people to God. The people of the land were to come together for a fast day.

(10) *"Cry unto the* LORD*."* Why? Because God is merciful. God is gracious. God wants to forgive. Our God is a wonderful God. They were to come to Him in this time of difficulty, and He would hear and answer their prayer.

Joel has given a warning to these people, and he has given them these injunctions. These are the things they are to do if they want the blessing of God upon them.

LOOKING TO THE DAY OF THE LORD (PRELUDE)

In a masterly way, Joel now moves from the local situation, this plague of locusts, down to the end of the age and the Day of the Lord.

Alas for the day! for the day of the LORD **is at hand, and as a destruction from the Almighty shall it come [Joel 1:15].**

"Alas for the day!" What day are you talking about, Joel? "For the day of the LORD is at hand, and as a destruction from the Almighty shall it come." Like a little model, a little adumbration of that which is coming in the future, this local plague of locusts was a warning, a picture of the coming Day of the Lord. It should have alerted the people.

Joel is now going to tell them about something in the future. That which was coming in the future, the thing which had been promised to David, was a kingdom. David would be raised up to rule over that Kingdom. War would cease, and there would be peace on the earth. All the prophets spoke about that, but they also spoke about what Joel is saying here—the coming of the Day of the Lord.

The Day of the Lord must be understood in contrast to the other days which are mentioned in Scripture. You and I are living today in what Scripture calls *man's day*. It began with Nebuchadnezzar, and the Lord Jesus labeled it "the times of the Gentiles." He said, ". . . Jerusalem shall be trodden down of the Gentiles, until the times of the Gentiles be fulfilled" (Luke 21:24). We are living in a man's day. Man is the one who makes the judgments today. We appeal to the Supreme Court, but we do not appeal to God. We have forgotten Him altogether. His name is just a word to swear by and to blaspheme.

Dr. Lewis Sperry Chafer makes this comment concerning man's day: "This theme, obscured at times by translators, is referred to but once in the New Testament, namely, 1 Corinthians 4:3, which reads, 'But with me it is a very small thing that I should be judged of you, or of man's judgment, yea, I judge not mine own self.' Now in this passage the phrase, 'man's judgment' is really a reference to human opinion current in this age, which might properly and literally be translated, 'man's day.'"

We are living in the day of man. Believe me, humanism abounds today. Man believes he can solve the problems of the world, but what has man really done? He has gotten the world into an awful mess right now. Every new politician who comes along thinks he has the answer. My friend, they do not have the answers; man cannot solve the problems of this world. I understand there have been some admissions in the cloakrooms of our own government and the chancelleries of the great nations of the world that man is incapable of solving the problems of the world today.

Scripture speaks of another day that is coming—the *Day of the Lord Jesus Christ*. Paul wrote in 1 Corinthians 1:7–8: "So that ye come behind in no gift; waiting for the coming of our Lord Jesus Christ: who shall also confirm you unto the end, that ye may be blameless in the day of our Lord Jesus Christ." What is the Day of the Lord Jesus Christ?

It is the day when He will come to take His church out of this world, and then the church will come before the judgment seat of Christ. My life verse is Philippians 1:6 which reads, "Being confident of this very thing, that he which hath begun a good work in you will perform it until the *day of Jesus Christ*" (italics mine). He is going to keep us until that day when He takes us out of the world and we appear before Him to see whether we receive a reward or not.

Both the Old and the New Testament speak of the *Day of the Lord.* Second Thessalonians 2:2 tells us, "That ye be not soon shaken in mind, or be troubled, neither by spirit, nor by word, nor by letter as from us, as that the day of Christ is at hand." The Thessalonian believers were afraid that they would miss the Rapture. Our translation of this verse is an unfortunate one—the word *Christ* should have been translated as "Lord"—in other words, "as the day of the Lord is at hand." Paul is assuring the believers that they will not go through the Day of the Lord.

Joel will make very clear what the Day of the Lord is. He will say that the Day of the Lord is a dark, gloomy, and difficult day. The Hebrew viewpoint was that they would enter immediately into the Kingdom—that life would be a breeze with no problems at all. But Joel says that the Day of the Lord begins with night, with darkness. That darkness is the Great Tribulation period. It will be like this locust plague that has come with its four bands of locusts like the four horsemen of the Apocalypse who will ride in the Great Tribulation period. Then the Day of the Lord will include the coming of Christ to the earth to establish His Kingdom. Then His people will enter into the sunshine of His presence. That was the Old Testament hope; that was the thing the Old Testament taught.

My friend, you can see how important it is to study all of the Bible. One man wrote to me to explain what he thought the Day of the Lord was. He wrote several pages, giving Scripture after Scripture, but he never gave one verse from Joel. He didn't understand that Joel is the very key. Joel was the first of the writing prophets. You cannot say the Day of the Lord is something other than what Joel says it is; it must fit into the program which he describes. All the prophets who came after him used this term many times. "The Day of the Lord" occurs about seventy-five times in the entire Bible; "the day of the LORD" occurs five times and "that day" one time in the Book of Joel. All of the prophets have a great deal to say about the Day of the Lord, and we need to recognize that it is a technical term which is defined and used consistently in Scripture.

To summarize, there is (1) man's day, the day in which we are living now; (2) the Day of the Lord Jesus Christ, when He will take the church out of this world; then (3) the Day of the Lord beginning with the Great Tribulation period. After all, we label the different days of the week: Monday, Tuesday, Wednesday, and so on. God has labeled these different periods of time also. This is not something men thought of, but it is what the Word of God teaches.

I should say that the Day of the Lord is not the same as the Lord's Day that is mentioned in Revelation 1:10. The Lord's Day is the first day of the week, which the New Testament makes very clear. Many people say the Day of the Lord and the Lord's Day are the same just because they use the same two words. That is ridiculous—as ridiculous as saying there is no difference between a chestnut horse and a horse chestnut. If you take two words and turn them around, you get something altogether different. In the one you've got a nut, and in the other you've got a horse! The Day of the Lord and the Lord's Day are two different things.

Is not the meat cut off before our eyes, yea, joy and gladness from the house of our God? [Joel 1:16].

Joel continues talking about this plague of locusts. There was no more joy and gladness in the house of God. I have had the privilege in the past few years of my ministry of speaking in the great pulpits of this country and at many of the great Bible conferences. I have noted that there is a sadness in congregations as they come together today. In many places I have found that at the first service there is an air of expectancy. You can feel it, the air is charged with it, but there is no note of gladness. At some meetings in Florida, a man with the FBI said to me, "I've been watching your method. I've noted that you get up before a congregation, and you slide very quietly and slowly into a funny story to get the people into a good humor." I said, "You've noticed that?" And he said, "Yes, and I think I know why you do it. I think you're doing it because there is a low level of joy among the people today." I told the man that he was right. The joy was gone in Israel, and today, even when we have everything, there is no joy in our services.

> **The seed is rotten under their clods, the garners are laid desolate, the barns are broken down; for the corn is withered [Joel 1:17].**

"The seed is rotten under their clods." The grain couldn't even come up, because the locusts had just gnawed off the shoots even with the ground. "The garners are laid desolate"—they could not fill up the granary.

> **How do the beasts groan! the herds of cattle are perplexed, because they have no pasture; yea, the flocks of sheep are made desolate.**

> **O Lord, to thee will I cry: for the fire hath devoured the pastures of the wilderness, and the flame hath burned all the trees of the field [Joel 1:18-19].**

The locusts have their own scorched earth policy. It was just as if the ground had been entirely burned off.

> **The beasts of the field cry also unto thee: for the rivers of waters are dried up, and the fire hath devoured the pastures of the wilderness [Joel 1:20].**

This was a very terrible, treacherous time. Even the animal world—both the animals in the barnyard and the wild animals out yonder in the forest—were being affected by this plague. It was a judgment that touched all life in that land in that day, and it becomes a picture of the Day of the Lord that is coming.

CHAPTER 2

THEME: Looking to the Day of the Lord; God's plea;
promise of deliverance; promise of the Holy Spirit

This chapter continues the prelude which was begun in 1:15, and,
of course, continues the theme.

LOOKING TO THE DAY OF THE LORD

You recall that God had promised David a kingdom, and that wonderful future kingdom became the theme song of all the prophets after
David. The great message is that the millennial Kingdom is coming
upon this earth. As we read the prophets, it sounds like a stuck record
as one after another looks forward to it.

Now Joel, the first of the writing prophets, makes it clear that the
Day of the Lord—which includes the millennial Kingdom—will not
be all peaches and cream. Before the millennial Kingdom (when the
Lord Jesus will be ruling on this earth), there will be a time which the
Lord Jesus defined as the Great Tribulation period. Chapter 2 will
make this clear to us.

> **Blow ye the trumpet in Zion, and sound an alarm in my
> holy mountain: let all the inhabitants of the land trem-
> ble: for the day of the LORD cometh, for it is nigh at hand
> [Joel 2:1].**

"The day of the LORD cometh." Let me remind you that Joel is the first
of the writing prophets, and he looks way down through the centuries
and sees the Day of the Lord. It begins with darkness, that is, with
judgment. Then Christ comes to the earth and establishes His Kingdom. Malachi speaks of Him as the ". . . Sun of righteousness [who
will] arise with healing in his wings . . ." (Mal. 4:2).

"Blow ye the trumpet in Zion, and sound an alarm in my holy mountain." "Zion" and "my holy mountain" refer to Jerusalem. He says they should blow the trumpet and sound an alarm. It is important for us to understand the significance of the trumpet. One needs to have a full-orbed view of the Bible so that on any given subject we are able to put our thinking down on all four corners and make an induction. Understanding the background will enable us to appreciate what the writer is saying.

What is the significance of the blowing of the trumpet? Back in the Book of Numbers we learn that when the children of Israel started through the wilderness, God commanded them to make two silver trumpets. He gave the instructions to Moses: "And the LORD spake unto Moses, saying, Make thee two trumpets of silver; of a whole piece shalt thou make them: that thou mayest use them for the calling of the assembly, and for the journeying of the camps" (Num. 10:1–2). When Israel was in the wilderness, God used the trumpets to move them on the wilderness march. The first blowing of the trumpet was a signal that everybody should get ready to march. When the pillar of cloud would lift and move out, they would take down the tabernacle. Then immediately the trumpet would sound again, and Moses and Aaron would move up front ahead of the tribe of Judah, and the ark would go out ahead with them. You will remember that Israel was encamped around the tabernacle on all four sides, three tribes on each side. Now each section would move out in turn, signaled by the blowing of the trumpets. Actually, to get the whole camp on the march, the trumpets were blown seven different times.

Now when we come to Revelation, the final book of the Bible, we find the blowing of the trumpets again. Although some expositors feel that this is in relation to the church, there is no blowing of the trumpet for the church. The sound of the trumpet at the time of the Rapture (1 Thess. 4:16) will be the shout of Christ Himself: "For the Lord himself shall descend from heaven with a shout, with the voice of the archangel, and with the trump of God . . ."—His voice will be like a trumpet.

The seven trumpets in Revelation have nothing to do with the church. The church will have been completed and will have been taken out of the world. The seven trumpets are identified with the nation Israel, just as there were the seven trumpet calls in the wilderness march.

If we turn back to the Book of Numbers, we will see that the different trumpet calls meant certain definite things. They were a way of giving instructions to Israel: "And when they shall blow with them, all the assembly shall assemble themselves to thee at the door of the tabernacle of the congregation. And if they blow but with one trumpet, then the princes, which are heads of the thousands of Israel, shall gather themselves unto thee. When ye blow an alarm, then the camps that lie on the east parts shall go forward. When ye blow an alarm the second time, then the camps that lie on the south side shall take their journey: they shall blow an alarm for their journeys. But when the congregation is to be gathered together, ye shall blow, but ye shall not sound an alarm" (Num. 10:3–7). Then he gives instructions for the time they will be in the Promised Land: "And if ye go to war in your land against the enemy that oppresseth you, then ye shall blow an alarm with the trumpets; and ye shall be remembered before the LORD your God, and ye shall be saved from your enemies" (Num. 10:9). During the time of war the trumpet would call the men of war to defend their country when an enemy was coming.

Now here in Joel's prophecy he says, "Blow ye the trumpet in Zion, and sound an *alarm* in my holy mountain." Why? "Let all the inhabitants of the land tremble: for the *day of the LORD cometh*, for it is nigh [near] at hand." You see, after the Lord has called His church out of the world, He will turn again to the nation of Israel, which becomes the object of worldwide anti-Semitism. This is the beginning of the Day of the Lord.

Now in this second chapter, Joel is going to give a blending of the plague of locusts together with the threat of the Assyrian army and then look down the avenue of time into the future and the Day of the Lord. Of course the liberal theologian would say this refers simply to the locust plague and the local situation. He would like to dismiss a great deal of meaning from the Word of God. The other extreme view is to say this refers only to the Great Tribulation period.

I think we need to see that in Joel there is a marvelous blending. He moves right out of the locust plague to the Day of the Lord which is way out yonder in the future. You recall that was the practice of the prophets to speak into a local situation and then move out into the future Day of the Lord—which includes the Tribulation period and the Millennium.

The local situation was the plague of locusts, and in the near future the Assyrian army was coming down: "But I will remove far off from you the *northern army*" (v. 20). I think it would be rather ridiculous to call a plague of locusts the northern army, but the plague of locusts was a picture of the Assyrian army that would be coming out of the north, and the Assyrian army becomes the picture of the enemy which will be coming out of the north in the last days. As we see in chapters 38 and 39 of Ezekiel, the northern army refers to present-day Russia which will invade Israel. In fact, Russia's coming will usher in the last half of the Great Tribulation period.

Let me remind you that the Day of the Lord is not a twenty-four hour day, but a period of time. The apostle Paul used it in that sense when he said, ". . . now is the accepted time; behold, now is the *day* of salvation" (2 Cor. 6:2, italics mine), speaking of the age of grace.

Let me repeat that the Day of the Lord is different from the Lord's Day, which refers to the first day of the week. Although the two words are the same, their arrangement makes all the difference. The difference is as great as between a chestnut horse and a horse chestnut!

Now Joel will put down God's definition that will condition and limit the prophets who will speak in the future. After this, all of them will speak into this period. It is interesting to find that none of them contradict each other, even though some of the prophets didn't know what the others were prophesying.

A day of darkness and of gloominess, a day of clouds and of thick darkness, as the morning spread upon the mountains: a great people and a strong; there hath not been ever the like, neither shall be any more after it, even to the years of many generations [Joel 2:2].

This is the same period about which the Lord Jesus said, "For then shall be great tribulation, such as was not since the beginning of the world to this time, no, nor ever shall be" (Matt. 24:21). The Great Tribulation opens the Day of the Lord because that is the way the Hebrew day opens; it begins in the evening at the time of darkness. I have a notion that when the plague of locusts came over the land, they would actually darken the sky because there would be so many of them. And the Day of the Lord will begin with darkness.

A fire devoureth before them; and behind them a flame burneth: the land is as the garden of Eden before them, and behind them a desolate wilderness; yea, and nothing shall escape them [Joel 2:3].

Before the plague of locusts came, the earth looked like the Garden of Eden. Everything was green with rich, luxurious foliage. The land was beautiful. After the locusts left, there was not a bit of green to be seen. It looked as if a fire had swept over the land.

The Day of the Lord will be the same in that it will be a time of destruction. When the four horsemen of the Apocalypse ride through this world, there will be war and famine and death. In one fell swoop, one fourth of the population will be wiped out, and at another time, one third of the population will be destroyed.

The appearance of them is as the appearance of horses; and as horsemen, so shall they run [Joel 2:4].

As I indicated before, the head of the locust resembles a horse's head, and the Italian word for locust means "little horse"; the German word means "hay horse." As the horse eats hay, the locusts would eat up everything green. Joel is describing the locust plague and is beginning to make application of it to the Day of the Lord.

Like the noise of chariots on the tops of mountains shall they leap, like the noise of a flame of fire that devoureth the stubble, as a strong people set in battle array.

Before their face the people shall be much pained: all faces shall gather blackness [Joel 2:5-6].

"All faces shall gather blackness"—that is, they will be scorched.

They shall run like mighty men; they shall climb the wall like men of war; and they shall march every one on his ways, and they shall not break their ranks [Joel 2:7].

In the Book of Proverbs it says this: "The locusts have no king, yet go they forth all of them by bands" (Prov. 30:27). They don't need a king or a leader—each one knows his place. They come in bands. When Joel describes four different groups of locusts here, I believe he is describing the movement of a great army—an army of locusts. In the last days, there will come against that land another enemy, and it will come like a locust plague. This is a preparation for the Book of Revelation in which the apostle John writes of a locust plague that will take place on the earth during the first woe which follows the blowing of the fifth trumpet: "And the fifth angel sounded, and I saw a star fall from heaven unto the earth: and to him was given the key of the bottomless pit. And he opened the bottomless pit; and there arose a smoke out of the pit, as the smoke of a great furnace; and the sun and the air were darkened by reason of the smoke of the pit. And there came out of the smoke locusts upon the earth: and unto them was given power, as the scorpions of the earth have power. And it was commanded them that they should not hurt the grass of the earth, neither any green thing, neither any tree; but only those men which have not the seal of God in their foreheads" (Rev. 9:1-4).

This is an unusual locust that will not attack anything green—that is all the normal locust would attack. They did not attack human beings. But these locusts will attack "only those men which have not the seal of God in their foreheads."

It will be such a terrifying time that men will seek death and will not be able to find it; that is, they will not be able to commit suicide: "And to them it was given that they should not kill them, but that they should be tormented five months: and their torment was as the torment of a scorpion, when he striketh a man. And in those days shall men seek death, and shall not find it; and shall desire to die, and death shall flee from them" (Rev. 9:5–6).

Now notice this description of the locusts: "And the shapes of the locusts were like unto horses prepared unto battle; and on their heads were as it were crowns like gold, and their faces were as the faces of men. And they had hair as the hair of women, and their teeth were as the teeth of lions" (Rev. 9:7–8). My friend, that is an unusual type of locust! This plague will take place during the Great Tribulation.

You can see that Joel, way back here at the beginning of the writing prophets, prepares the ground for the apostle John to come later and give the detailed description of the locusts as they will appear in the Day of the Lord.

May I just say that this is the reason I think it is tragic today to find so many people who have just been converted who think they are qualified to start a Bible class. What books do they like to start to teach? Usually you will find they choose either the Gospel of John or the Book of Revelation. In my judgment, that is not the place to begin with new believers. I believe Matthew is the key book to the Bible. Until you understand Matthew, I don't think you will quite get the message of the Gospel of John and I *know* you will miss the message of the Book of Revelation. And this little prophet Joel, who has been by and large ignored, sheds a great deal of light on the last days which he calls the Day of the Lord.

When Joel writes: "They shall run like mighty men; they shall climb the wall like men of war," he is beginning to move from the local locust plague into the future which he has labeled the Day of the Lord.

In the next verse we will see that he *is* talking about the Day of the Lord.

Neither shall one thrust another; they shall walk every one in his path: and when they fall upon the sword, they shall not be wounded.

They shall run to and fro in the city; they shall run upon the wall, they shall climb up upon the houses; they shall enter in at the windows like a thief.

> The earth shall quake before them; the heavens shall
> tremble: the sun and the moon shall be dark, and the
> stars shall withdraw their shining [Joel 2:8-10].

Obviously this is more than a local locust plague or else Joel is exaggerating; the prophets spoke God's Word as He gave it to them—they didn't exaggerate. This is the same picture that John gives us in the Book of Revelation.

> And the LORD shall utter his voice before his army: for
> his camp is very great: for he is strong that executeth his
> word: for the day of the LORD is great and very terrible;
> and who can abide it? [Joel 2:11].

This is the third time Joel has mentioned the Day of the Lord.

"Who can abide it?" This is very much the same as Jesus said, "Except those days should be shortened, there should no flesh be saved" (Matt. 24:22). And Joel asks, "Who can abide it?" Well, John gives the answer in Revelation. In chapter 7 he says that God will shut down the forces of nature, withholding the winds from blowing (which are judgments of God upon the earth) until the two great companies of the redeemed are sealed and made secure. If God's people are going to make it through the terrible time of tribulation, they will have to be sealed. When Joel asks, "Who can abide it?" the "it" is the Day of the Lord, which begins in darkness, the night of the Great Tribulation.

GOD'S PLEA

Now the question is: What can a sinner do in a period like this? Well, Joel gives the answer for that:

> Therefore also now, saith the LORD, turn ye even to me
> with all your heart, and with fasting, and with weeping,
> and with mourning [Joel 2:12].

"Turn ye even to me with all your heart." The word *turn* means "repent." God says to His people whose hearts are turned from Him, "Repent." Repent means primarily to change your mind. You indicate a change of mind by turning around. It is true there may be some shedding of tears along with the repentance, but that is only a by-product of repentance. Repentance really means to change your mind.

When I first entered the ministry, I went to my home church in Nashville as a pastor. I had some of the most wonderful people in that church—they had to be wonderful to put up with me! It was my first pastorate, and I was as green as grass. I could be very serious but also rather frivolous. I was not married yet; so I would take off to go to Atlanta, Georgia, or to Memphis, Tennessee, because I knew some girls in both places.

The man who was humanly responsible for my entering the ministry was in that church. He had arranged a loan for me because I was a poor boy with no money. Also he had helped me get a job. He was like a father to me, and I loved him as a father.

One day I went to the bank to tell him something that I had in mind. He let me know immediately that my idea was not a very good idea, as many of mine have not been. He let me know in no uncertain terms. That angered me, so I turned and started out the door. When I got to the street, I thought, "This is not right. I owe this man a great deal." So I turned around and went back. Do you know why I turned around? Because it came into my mind and into my heart that I ought to do it. When I got back to his office I saw tears coming from his eyes. By the way, when my wife and I were in Nashville on our honeymoon, he said to her, "I don't know much about you, whether or not you get angry quickly, but Vernon has a very high temper, and don't both of you get angry at the same time!" Well, one of things that made my wife so attractive to me was her mild, even temper, and she has put up with a whole lot from this poor preacher! But the day I returned to his office I repented of the thing I had done, and I manifested it in turning and going back to him.

Now when God says, "Turn ye even to me with all your heart," He means to repent, and the by-product of it will be fasting, weeping, and mourning. Unfortunately, a great many people think that if they go down to an altar and shed enough tears, they are converted. Well, I went through that process as a boy and found it to be absolutely meaningless.

And rend your heart, and not your garments, and turn unto the Lord your God: for he is gracious and merciful, slow to anger, and of great kindness, and repenteth him of the evil [Joel 2:13].

You see, this was to be a heart experience, not some outward gesture. Actually, the Mosaic Law forbade the priest from tearing his garments. Repentance was not to be shown by being a fanatic. The tear was to be in the heart.

"And turn unto the Lord your God" is repentance.

Now he gives the reason for turning to the Lord: "For he is gracious and merciful, slow to anger, and of great kindness, and repenteth him of the evil." In the Books of Exodus and Jonah, I deal more thoroughly with the question of what it means when God repents. When Israel was in Egypt, it looked as if God changed His mind. He sent plague after plague to Egypt to give Pharaoh the opportunity to repent and turn to Him, but he didn't. Also in Jonah's day, God sent Jonah to preach to the Ninevites that He would destroy the city. However, Ninevah repented and turned to God; so God did not destroy the city. It looked as if God had changed His mind after He said that He would destroy the city, but He did not change His mind. God is immutable. He is always gracious; He is always merciful, and He is always slow to anger.

My friend, you can always depend upon God. He never changes, He is immutable; but when a sinner repents and turns to Him, God says in effect, "You were under My judgment, and I was going to judge you, but now that you have turned to Me, I will not judge you." God is always gracious and ready to forgive.

Who knoweth if he will return and repent, and leave a blessing behind him; even a meat offering and a drink offering unto the Lord your God? [Joel 2:14].

In other words, "The Lord will bless you again in the field and in the vineyard, and you will have a drink offering and you'll have a meat offering to bring to Him."

Incidentally, the drink offering is mentioned here; yet there is no instruction in Leviticus for a drink offering. The drink offering was poured on the other offerings and became a part of them. When it was poured on the sacrifice, it went up in steam on the hot coals. The apostle Paul, you recall, said that he wanted his life to be like that— just a drink offering on the sacrifice of Christ.

> **Blow the trumpet in Zion, sanctify a fast, call a solemn assembly [Joel 2:15].**

At the beginning of this chapter we saw that the blowing of the trumpet was used to call an assembly and also to sound an alarm. In verse 1 it was to sound an alarm. Now here at verse 15 it is to call an assembly. The people were to be brought together to hear God's message so that they might have the opportunity to turn to God. He is gracious and good, and He is willing to accept them.

"Sanctify a fast, call a solemn assembly." As we have seen, in the Mosaic system God gave His people only feast days. They were to come before Him with rejoicing. But now that they are in sin and rebellion against Him and have turned from Him, they are to fast and come before Him in a solemn assembly.

My friend, the only way we can come to Him is to come as sinners wanting to turn from our sins. If you have been turning *from* God and now will turn *to* God, all you have to do is call upon Him and He will save you. ". . . Believe on the Lord Jesus Christ, and thou shalt be saved . . ." (Acts 16:31). You don't need to do anything but that. You don't need to join a church, go through a ceremony, or promise Him something. You simply turn as a sinner to Christ for His mercy.

It is interesting that the word for preaching or evangelizing or heralding the gospel is a word that means trumpet. The trumpet call of the New Testament is the gospel message that we are to get out to the world. "Blow the trumpet in Zion." This is to call a solemn assembly.

When people respond to an altar call and come down to the front of the church, it is a solemn moment. They are testifying that they are turning to God from sin. That is serious business and should not be done lightly. However, I emphasize again that it is not merely going to the altar of a church that constitutes real repentance.

A lovely young couple in Memphis responded to an altar call and came down to the front of the church after a message I had given. I went down to talk to them and asked them, "Is this the first time you have responded to a call?"

"No, we come down every Sunday."

"Then why do you come down to the altar?"

"Because we want all that God has for us."

"Do you think you will get that by just coming down here?"

"We hope so."

"Let me ask you another question. Do you think you have it now?"

"No, we don't."

"Then I would get a little discouraged if I were you. Maybe this isn't the way it is to be done. Maybe you are trying man's way, and God has another way. God wants to be good and gracious to you, and He wants to save you, but you must come to Him His way. No man comes to the Father but by the Lord Jesus Christ. He is the only door to heaven." Jesus Himself said, "I am the door: by me if any man enter in, he shall be saved, and shall go in and out, and find pasture" (John 10:9).

> **Gather the people, sanctify the congregation, assemble the elders, gather the children, and those that suck the breasts: let the bridegroom go forth of his chamber, and the bride out of her closet [Joel 2:16].**

"Gather the children, and those that suck the breasts" sounds as if the little children were to be taken care of in the nursery so their mothers could give this assembly their full attention. Notice that even the bridegroom is to go to the assembly. When a man was married in Israel, he was excused from going to war for one year. In fact, he was excused from a lot of duties so he could get acquainted with his bride. I guess that was an advantage of getting married! However, God is saying here that everybody is to be gathered together—even the bridegroom and the bride if they are on their honeymoon.

> **Let the priests, the ministers of the LORD, weep between the porch and the altar, and let them say, Spare thy people, O LORD, and give not thine heritage to reproach, that the heathen should rule over them: wherefore should they say among the people, Where is their God? [Joel 2:17].**

The priests and the ministers of the Lord are to weep. Joel is in Jerusalem, you see; he is a prophet of the southern kingdom.

They were to pray, "Spare thy people, O LORD, and give not thine heritage to reproach, that the heathen [nations] should rule over them." Israel has been scattered throughout the world to this day. Although they have a nation and a government and a flag, they are still pretty well subject to the nations of the world. As I write this, they are caught in the oil slick which is causing them a great deal of trouble, and it will continue to cause trouble because they are not back in the land today in fulfillment of prophecy. When God puts them back into the land, there will be no problem relative to the oil situation.

Golda Meir made a statement which inferred that Moses had made a mistake. She said something like this: "Imagine! Moses led all of our people around through the wilderness for forty years and brought them to the only place in this area that has no oil!" Well, if she believed the Old Testament, she would know that they were led by a pillar of fire by night and a pillar of cloud by day, and that God had a definite purpose for keeping them from settling on land that was rich with oil. They would never have gotten their land back—that's for sure! Actually what Israel needs is not oil but water. They don't have enough water because the judgment of God is upon them. Moses made no mistake because he was following the orders of God, and certainly God makes no mistakes.

"Wherefore should they say among the people, Where is their God?" They were wondering what was happening to them. And today that is still their question. In Israel I talked with a sharp young Jewish fellow at the King David Hotel. He said, "If it is as you say that we are God's chosen people, why doesn't He intervene for us today?" I told him very candidly, "Because right now, you are not with God. Until you come back in repentance to Him, He is not dealing with you as His chosen people. Today God is doing a new thing: He is calling out from among your people and my people—Jews and Gentiles—a people to His name. You are just not up to date with God. You are going way back to the Mosaic system which is outmoded. The latest thing, the newest model, is the church of the Lord Jesus Christ." You see, God is inviting "whosoever will" to trust Christ and become a part of the new organism which He calls the church.

PROMISE OF DELIVERANCE

Now he is definitely moving into the future. Notice the time-word "Then." It will appear several times in this chapter.

Then will the LORD be jealous for his land, and pity his people [Joel 2:18].

In the Olivet Discourse (see Matt. 24—25), the Lord Jesus used the word *then* to advance in time the happenings that will take place in the Great Tribulation period. At the end of the Great Tribulation period, just before the Lord returns to this earth, *then* will He be jealous for His land and pity His people.

Yea, the LORD will answer and say unto his people, Behold, I will send you corn, and wine, and oil, and ye shall be satisfied therewith: and I will no more make you a reproach among the heathen [Joel 2:19].

At that time the Lord will give them corn and wine and oil; they will be satisfied, and no longer will they be a reproach among the heathen. Even the most radical radical today would not say that this is being fulfilled now. The largest population of Israel is not in the land. There are more Jews in New York City than there are in Israel. And there is a great company of them even in Russia. This is not being fulfilled at this time. This still looks forward to the future. It is definitely the period known as the Day of the Lord, which will begin with darkness and move on into the dawn of the Millennium, past man's rebellion that breaks out on the earth, and on to the beginning of the eternal Kingdom. From here on we are bottled into that particular period.

But I will remove far off from you the northern army, and will drive him into a land barren and desolate, with his face toward the east sea, and his hinder part toward the utmost sea, and his stink shall come up, and his ill savour shall come up, because he hath done great things [Joel 2:20].

"I will remove far off from you the northern army" certainly is not talking about locusts but an army coming down from the north. This was partially fulfilled when Assyria came down and took the northern kingdom, but God miraculously delivered the southern kingdom from them. It was another hundred years before the southern kingdom went into captivity—and then it was to the Babylonians, not the Assyrians.

However, there is still a future fulfillment of the removal of the northern army. This is given in more detail in Ezekiel 38—39. In the Great Tribulation period Russia will come down from the north, but God will deliver Israel. The description given here fits the description of the Battle of Armageddon. "And will drive him into a land barren and desolate, with his face toward the east sea, and his hinder part toward the utmost sea, and his stink shall come up, and his ill savour shall come up, because he hath done great things." The Sea of Galilee is on one side and the Mediterranean Sea is on the other side of the Valley of Esdraelon where Armageddon will take place. God will intervene as we have seen in Ezekiel. He will destroy this enemy that comes from the north, and He does it to glorify His name.

God is glorified when He judges sin just as much as He is when He saves a sinner. That is hard for us to believe; it is a bitter pill for man to swallow. God is holy, and a holy, righteous God is going to judge. Every one of the prophets says that. The Word of God has a lot to say about the judgment of God. But He doesn't like to judge. We have already seen that He is gracious and merciful and slow to anger. Judgment is a strange work for God. That is why He holds out His hands all the day long and asks us to come to Him. When people refuse to turn to Him, He must judge them in His righteousness and in His holiness.

This is true even for the children of God. When we do wrong, if we do not judge ourselves, God must judge us. He chastens us to bring us back to Himself. To be honest with you, I have had some chastening from the Lord. I want to stick very close to my Heavenly Father because, I can tell you, I don't enjoy the chastening of the Lord.

Fear not, O land; be glad and rejoice: for the LORD will do great things [Joel 2:21].

The Tribulation period will lead to the coming of Christ to earth to establish His Kingdom. Today that land is still under a curse. They need water. The land is far from being a Garden of Eden. Anyone who has driven from Jerusalem to Jericho will have to admit it is just as desolate as the desert in Arizona and California.

You will notice that the church is not in this picture. Neither do we find the church in the Olivet Discourse nor in the Book of Revelation after chapter 4. The believers have been raptured, and there is no longer a church on earth. And when the church gets to heaven it will no longer be called the church (*ekklesia,* meaning "called out"), but the figure changes and the believers will be called the *bride* of Christ.

Be not afraid, ye beasts of the field: for the pastures of the wilderness do spring, for the tree beareth her fruit, the fig tree and the vine do yield their strength [Joel 2:22].

This day has not come yet.

> **Be glad then, ye children of Zion, and rejoice in the LORD your God: for he hath given you the former rain moderately, and he will cause to come down for you the rain, the former rain, and the latter rain in the first month [Joel 2:23].**

Who are the "children of Zion"? Of course they are the people of the southern kingdom—that is where Zion is located. You and I may sing lustily, "We're marching to Zion," but we are not marching to the Zion here upon this earth.

When he speaks of the "rain," he is talking about literal rain. In verse 28 Joel will make application of it in the pouring out of the Holy Spirit, but he is referring to literal rain in this verse. The former rain came in October, and the latter rain came in April. There are other passages in the Bible that speak of the former and the latter rains which were quite literal rains in the land of Israel (see Lev. 26:3–4; Deut. 11:14–17; 1 Kings 8:35–36; Jer. 3:3; Hos. 6:3).

Before I went over to Israel, I heard that the latter rain was returning to that land. Well, I have been over there in April, and it rained a little. But, gracious, I don't think people would call that the kind of rain which the Lord is talking about. In former days they really had rain. All those rugged hills of that land were covered with trees. The enemies came in and denuded the land, and today they are trying to set out trees, but they are having trouble making those trees grow because there is not enough of the latter rain. Joel is talking about these literal rains—H_2O—which God has promised in the future.

> **And the floors shall be full of wheat, and the vats shall overflow with wine and oil.**

> **And I will restore to you the years that the locust hath eaten, the cankerworm, and the caterpillar, and the palmerworm, my great army which I sent among you [Joel 2:24–25].**

"I will restore to you the years that the locust hath eaten." There have been a great many sermons preached on this, spiritualizing this passage. And it certainly can be used as an application since it states a great principle. We find the same thought in the Book of Revelation where God says, ". . . Behold, I make all things new . . ." (Rev. 21:5). He is speaking of the New Jerusalem in this chapter. Those of the church, the sinners who have trusted Christ, are going to be there. He tells us how wonderful it will be and about the fact that He will wipe away all tears from our eyes. What a change that will be! There are a lot of tears in this old world. I rejoice that He will make all things new.

I don't know about you, but I can say that I am not satisfied with my life down here. I have never preached the sermon I have wanted to preach—I wish I could do it. I have had it in my heart and in my mind, but somehow I have never been able to preach as well as I have wanted to. I have never been the husband that I have really wanted to be. I wish that I could have been a much better husband to my wife. When I was sick, she and I went back over the days when we met and how we courted, and all that sort of thing. As I told her, I wish I could change many things which would make it lots more wonderful than it was. Neither have I been the father that I wanted to be. I have never really been the man that I have wanted to be. That is why I love Revelation 21:5: ". . . Behold, I make all things new. . . ." My Lord will say, "Vernon McGee, you didn't quite make it down there on the earth. You never really accomplished your goals. You were frustrated. You were limited. You were down there with that old sinful nature. Now I am going to make all things new. I'm going to give you a new scratch pad and a new pencil without an eraser. You can write it all out now. You can accomplish what you wanted to accomplish."

My friend, that will really make heaven *heaven* for a lot of us. We will be able to do the things and be the person that we have wanted to be down here. Oh, to be free from the hindrances of circumstances, of sin, of the environment, and even of heredity. What a glorious experience to be free of all this and to be in the presence of Christ! He will make all things new. He will restore the years that the locusts have eaten.

And ye shall eat in plenty, and be satisfied, and praise the name of the LORD your God, that hath dealt wondrously with you: and my people shall never be ashamed.

And ye shall know that I am in the midst of Israel, and that I am the LORD your God, and none else: and my people shall never be ashamed [Joel 2:26–27].

This will take place when he is "in the midst of Israel"; that is, when Christ has come to the earth and has established His Kingdom. At that time there will be a fulfillment of all the physical blessings which God has promised to the nation Israel. And the blessings in the Old Testament were largely physical blessings. God promised to bless the land so that they would have bumper crops and their cattle would thrive and multiply. Actually the spiritual blessings seem almost secondary. In contrast to this, the blessings God has promised the church are spiritual blessings—only. We have all spiritual blessings in Christ Jesus.

Even though the primary blessings to Israel were physical blessings, we come now to a passage which speaks of spiritual blessing to Israel. This is a very controversial passage of Scripture.

PROMISE OF THE HOLY SPIRIT

As we come to this section, it is important to keep in mind that we are in the prophecy of Joel that began with the record of a frightful locust plague which he compared to that which is coming in the future, which he calls the Day of the Lord. We have seen that the Day of the Lord will begin with the Tribulation period, after which Christ will come and establish His Kingdom on the earth. In verse 27 we have just read that the Lord at this time will be in the midst of them. Now let's see what He is going to do.

And it shall come to pass afterward, that I will pour out my spirit upon all flesh; and your sons and your daugh-

ters shall prophesy, your old men shall dream dreams, your young men shall see visions:

And also upon the servants and upon the handmaids in those days will I pour out my spirit.

And I will shew wonders in the heavens and in the earth, blood, and fire, and pillars of smoke.

The sun shall be turned into darkness, and the moon into blood, before the great and the terrible day of the LORD come.

And it shall come to pass, that whosoever shall call on the name of the LORD shall be delivered: for in mount Zion and in Jerusalem shall be deliverance, as the LORD hath said, and in the remnant whom the LORD shall call [Joel 2:28-32].

There are many wonderful things that we could say about this passage of Scripture. Dr. Charles L. Feinberg, a Jewish Christian, and an outstanding Hebrew scholar, has written a fine series of books on the Minor Prophets which have been very helpful to me. In *Joel, Amos, and Obadiah,* pp. 26–27, he calls attention to something that I had not known before: "Verses 28 through 32 form chapter 3 in the Hebrew text; and chapter 3 in the English translations is chapter 4 in the original. No one will be inclined to doubt that the disclosure of truth in 2:28–32 is of sufficient importance to warrant its appearing in a separate chapter." I certainly agree that these five verses are important enough to make them a separate chapter.

In understanding this prophecy, it is of utmost importance to note the time of fulfillment indicated in this passage: "And it shall come to pass *(afterward)*." Joel has been telling us about the coming Day of the Lord. As the first of the writing prophets, he introduced it, and he tells what is going to take place during that period. He has emphasized the fact that it will begin with the darkness of the Great Tribulation period (our Lord Jesus gave it that name). We noted the importance of the time sequence in Hosea. In chapter 3, verse 5 of that prophecy it is written: "Afterward shall the children of Israel return, and seek the LORD their God, and David their king; and shall fear the LORD and his goodness in the latter days." We identified the "latter days" as that time of the Great Tribulation period which ushers in the Kingdom by the coming of Christ to the earth, which is the beginning of the Millennium. This leads us to conclude that Joel is now speaking of a very definite period of time, that this prophecy is to be fulfilled during the Day of the Lord, after the night of the Great Tribulation period. Then God will pour out His Spirit upon all flesh.

Although Joel is the first of the writing prophets, he is not the only one to mention the pouring out of the Spirit. In Isaiah we read: "Until the spirit be poured upon us from on high, and the wilderness be a fruitful field, and the fruitful field be counted for a forest" (Isa. 32:15). He is speaking of the Kingdom which is coming on the earth, and the pouring out of the Spirit has reference to the Millennium. Of course none of the prophets spoke of the church age; all of them spoke of the last days in reference to the nation Israel.

Ezekiel 36:27 says this: "And I will put my spirit within you, and cause you to walk in my statutes, and ye shall keep my judgments, and do them." Then he continues, "And ye shall dwell in the land that I gave to your fathers; and ye shall be my people, and I will be your God" (Ezek. 36:28). Now he is talking to a particular people and a particular land—Israel. It is also a particular period of time when God will pour out His Spirit. Also Ezekiel says: "And shall put my spirit in you, and ye shall live, and I shall place you in your own land: then shall ye know that I the LORD have spoken it, and performed it, saith the LORD" (Ezek. 37:14). That's not all: "Neither will I hide my face any more from them: for I have poured out my spirit upon the house of Israel, saith the Lord GOD" (Ezek. 39:29).

Zechariah is one of the last of the writing prophets. He says, "And I will pour upon the house of David, and upon the inhabitants of Jerusalem, the spirit of grace and of supplications: and they shall look upon me whom they have pierced, and they shall mourn for him, as one mourneth for his only son, and shall be in bitterness for him, as one that is in bitterness for his firstborn" (Zech. 12:10).

Joel also makes it clear in the passage we are discussing—"And it shall come to pass, that whosoever shall call on the name of the LORD shall be delivered: for in *mount Zion* and in *Jerusalem* shall be deliverance"—that he refers to a certain spot on the map.

The question arises: What did Peter mean when he referred to this passage of Scripture on the Day of Pentecost? Did he mean that the prophecy of Joel was fulfilled? No, he didn't say that. He never claimed that this prophecy was fulfilled.

On the Day of Pentecost, when the Holy Spirit came upon the disciples they began to speak to Jews who had come to Jerusalem from all over the Roman Empire. Every man heard the message in his own tongue. These were not *unknown* tongues in which the disciples were speaking the message. Each tongue was the native tongue of one or more of the men who were gathered there from all over the Roman Empire and even beyond the empire.

Well, many believed, but others began to mock and say that the disciples were drunk—filled with new wine. So Simon Peter is the one who gets up to answer them. He acted as the spokesman for the group, and he gave an answer to the accusation that they were drunk. ". . . Ye men of Judaea, and all ye that dwell at Jerusalem, be this known unto you, and hearken to my words: For these are not drunken, as ye suppose, seeing it is but the third hour of the day" (Acts 2:14–15). Peter says you wouldn't find people drunk in the morning. (It's a little different in modern America—some people start drinking pretty early in the day.)

Peter continues, "But this is that which was spoken by the prophet Joel" (Acts 2:16). You will notice that Peter does not say that this is in *fulfillment* of what the prophet Joel said. All the Gospel writers and the apostle Paul are very clear when they say that something is the fulfillment of a prophecy. I couldn't begin to mention all of the passages. For examples, turn to Matthew 2:17–18: "Then was *fulfilled* that which was spoken by Jeremy the prophet, saying, In Rama was there a voice heard, lamentation, and weeping, and great mourning, Rachel weeping for her children, and would not be comforted, because they are *not*" (italics mine). That was a fulfillment of prophecy that had to do with incidents associated with the birth of Christ. Drop down to verse 23: "And he came and dwelt in a city called Nazareth: that it might be *fulfilled* which was spoken by the prophets, He shall be called a Nazarene" (italics mine). Or turn to Acts 13 to the sermon of Paul at Antioch in Pisidia. He speaks of the resurrection of Jesus Christ and says, "And we declare unto you glad tidings, how that the promise which was made unto the fathers, God hath *fulfilled* the same unto us their children, in that he hath raised up Jesus again; as it is also written in the second psalm, Thou art my Son, this day have I begotten thee" (Acts 13:32–33, italics mine). The Bible is very definite about fulfillment of prophecy.

What does Peter say in Acts 2:16? ". . . this is *that* which was spoken by the prophet Joel" (italics mine). He does not say it was a fulfillment of what Joel had predicted. Rather, he said, "This is *that*"—this is like that or similar to that. If you will go back in your mind to the Day of Pentecost, you will realize that Peter was not talking to Gentiles; he was speaking to Jews who were schooled in the Old Testament. They *knew* the Old Testament. They were Jews from all over the empire who had come to Jerusalem for the feast; they had traveled long distances because they were keeping what was required of them according to the Mosaic Law. Peter says to them in effect, "Don't mock, don't ridicule this thing which you see happening. This is like that which is going to take place in the Day of the Lord as it is told to us by the prophet Joel."

He quotes Joel's prophecy. "And it shall come to pass in the last days, saith God, I will pour out of my Spirit upon *all* flesh . . ." (Acts 2:17, italics mine). This is to occur in the last days. Then the Spirit of God will be poured out upon all flesh. Was that fulfilled on the Day of Pentecost? Hardly. It was experienced by those enumerated in the previous chapter. And three thousand were saved. Even if it had been three hundred thousand who were saved, it still would not have been a pouring out of the Spirit upon all flesh. It would still not have been a fulfillment of Joel's prophecy.

In effect, Peter is saying to them, "Don't mock at what you see happening. You ought to recognize from your own Word of God that

Joel says the day is coming when God will pour out His Spirit on all flesh. If it is poured out on a few people today, you ought not to be surprised at that."

Then Peter went on to quote the rest of Joel's prophecy regarding what would take place: "I will shew wonders in the heavens and in the earth, blood, and fire, and pillars of smoke. The sun shall be turned into darkness, and the moon into blood, before the great and terrible day of the LORD come" (vv. 30–31). Was that fulfilled on the Day of Pentecost? Of course not. There were no earthquakes, no changes in the sun and moon. These will occur on "that great and notable day of the Lord." Joel calls it, "the great and terrible day of the LORD." The Day of Pentecost was a great day, but it was not a terrible day. It was a wonderful day!

My friend, if we understand the Book of Joel, we will never come to the conclusion that Peter was saying that the prophecy of Joel was being fulfilled on the Day of Pentecost. Simon Peter was merely using Joel's prophecy as an introduction to answer those who were mocking.

Now the question arises: What was the *subject* of Simon Peter's message? On the Day of Pentecost the subject of Simon Peter's sermon was the resurrection of the Lord Jesus Christ. Now when he comes to his text, he uses Psalm 16:8–10, which prophesied the resurrection of Christ. Notice how he applies it to Christ: "This Jesus hath God raised up, whereof we all are witnesses. Therefore being by the right hand of God exalted, and having received of the Father the promise of the Holy Ghost, he hath shed forth this, which ye now see and hear (Acts 2:32–33).

The conclusion both in Joel and in Peter's address is, "And it shall come to pass, that whosoever shall call on the name of the LORD shall be delivered [Peter says, Shall be saved]." This is one of the many passages that causes me to make the statement that I think the greatest time of salvation is yet in the future. I believe God will save more of the human race than will be lost. I agree with Spurgeon who said that he believed God would win more to Himself than would be lost. When Christ comes to the earth to establish His Kingdom, there is going to be the greatest time of individuals turning to God that the world has ever seen. Also during the Tribulation period there will be a great turning to the Lord—much greater than there has been during the church age. The resurrection of Jesus Christ whom God has made both Lord and Christ is the whole point of Peter's sermon. He is not emphasizing the phenomenon they had witnessed. The important issue is coming to know Jesus Christ. Oh, my friend, don't be so occupied with having an experience that you miss coming to know Christ. What place does He occupy in your thinking, in your life, in your ministry?

This section of Joel's prophecy is all-important, but it is yet to be fulfilled.

CHAPTER 3

THEME: Looking at the Day of the Lord (postlude)

For, behold, in those days, and in that time, when I shall bring again the captivity of Judah and Jerusalem [Joel 3:1].

"**F**or, behold, in those days." What day? The Day of Pentecost? No, for He says, "when I shall bring again the captivity of Judah and Jerusalem." He did not bring them back at Pentecost; in fact, the Lord Jesus reversed the order when He said, ". . . ye shall be witnesses unto me both in Jerusalem, and in all Judaea, and in Samaria, and unto the uttermost part of the earth" (Acts 1:8). Instead of bringing the captivity back to Jerusalem, Christ, as head of the church, said to those who now have been born again and are in the body of believers, "Go to the ends of the earth. Take the message out that I am raised from the dead. Tell them that God is gracious and longsuffering and merciful, and that whosoever will call upon the name of the Lord will be saved."

The gospel seems so simple that a lot of smart people miss it today. How wonderful it is! All you do is believe. I want to say that I do not believe in a works salvation—that is obvious—but I do believe in a salvation that works. That is important to see. If you have been saved, you'll want to get the gospel out. If you don't want to, my friend, I'd question your faith—not your works, but your faith—because faith *works.*

I will also gather all nations, and will bring them down into the valley of Jehoshaphat, and will plead with them there for my people and for my heritage Israel, whom they have scattered among the nations, and parted my land [Joel 3:2].

"I will also gather all nations, and will bring them down into the valley of Jehoshaphat"—that is there at Jerusalem.

"And will plead with them there for my people and for my heritage Israel, whom they have scattered among the nations, and parted my land." Before the Lord Jesus comes again to the earth, believers will already have appeared before His judgment seat to see whether or not they are to receive a reward. When He comes to the earth, then He will judge to see who will enter the Kingdom. We have this marvelous prophecy here, but it is not found only in the Book of Joel. Joel is the first of the writing prophets, but all of the prophets mentioned it. One of the last prophets, Zechariah, said the same thing, "Sing and rejoice, O daughter of Zion: for, lo, I come, and I will dwell in the midst of thee, saith the LORD. And many nations shall be joined to the LORD in that day, and shall be my people: and I will dwell in the midst of thee, and thou shalt know that the LORD of hosts hath sent me unto thee" (Zech. 2:10–11). This is the same thing Joel told the people at the beginning. This was their great hope, their bright hope, that the Lord will come to establish His Kingdom on the earth and the Spirit will be poured out on all flesh.

And they have cast lots for my people; and have given a boy for an harlot; and sold a girl for wine, that they might drink [Joel 3:3].

This is an awful thing that Joel describes here. I get a little provoked sometimes with the Society for the Prevention of Cruelty to Animals which has come up with some unusual demands as to how we should treat animals. They are opposed to the foxhunt, although the fox generally gets away and they don't really need to worry about him at all; they also are opposed to all types of hunting and shooting of game. However, they haven't been down to the stockyards yet to stop the slaughter of cattle, because most of them like their porterhouse and sirloin steaks as well as their prime rib roast. But that is really not my point, because I agree that animals should not be mistreated and that they often suffer because of man's sin. The greatest cruelty today, however, is cruelty toward children. It is one of the most appalling things that is happening in our day. I read sometime ago of a mother who had co-habited with some no good, ne'er-do-well man who beat her little boy. A precious little boy—what a beautiful child he was at the beginning. But they also showed a picture of him near the end; he'd been beaten and mistreated and finally killed by that man! Actually, there was not much protest over that. The mistreatment of a dog has caused more furor in our communities than did the mistreatment of that child. Such cruelty toward children is one of the signs of the end of an age.

Why are so many children running away from home in this day? I think any parent who has a runaway child needs to get down on his knees before God and ask Him what he has done wrong. Someone will say, "Well, the child got in with the wrong crowd. We need the help of a psychologist." My friend, we don't need that—we need to read the Word of God. God says the evil day will come when "they have cast lots for my people; and have given a boy for an harlot." How many fathers today are setting the right example for their sons? "And sold a girl for wine, that they might drink." How many girls are being plunged into immorality because of liquor in their homes? One young girl, who had become a harlot and was arrested, was asked where she took her first drink. She said that it had been with her mother. God have mercy on a mother who would do a thing like that! Someone needs to speak out today in this so-called suave and sophisticated age that wants to think we are advancing in civilization. My friend, we are going down the tubes so fast it's making us dizzy.

> **Yea, and what have ye to do with me, O Tyre, and Zidon, and all the coasts of Palestine? will ye render me a recompence? and if ye recompense me, swiftly and speedily will I return your recompence upon your own head [Joel 3:4].**

God says that they have gone past the time and are unable to turn to Him sincerely.

> Because ye have taken my silver and my gold, and have
> carried into your temples my goodly pleasant things:
>
> The children also of Judah and the children of Jerusa-
> lem have ye sold unto the Grecians, that ye might re-
> move them far from their border [Joel 3:5–6].

Even at this time the children of Israel were being sold into slavery, yet this was before Rome had come to power.

> Behold, I will raise them out of the place whither ye
> have sold them, and will return your recompence upon
> your own head:
>
> And I will sell your sons and your daughters into the
> hand of the children of Judah, and they shall sell them
> to the Sabeans, to a people far off: for the LORD hath spo-
> ken it [Joel 3:7–8].

God's judgment of Tyre and Sidon, prophesied also by Ezekiel, Jeremiah, and Isaiah, has all been literally fulfilled.

> Proclaim ye this among the Gentiles; Prepare war, wake
> up the mighty men, let all the men of war draw near; let
> them come up:
>
> Beat your plowshares into swords, and your prun-
> inghooks into spears: let the weak say, I am strong [Joel
> 3:9–10].

"Beat your plowshares into swords, and your pruninghooks into spears." Someone will say, "I thought the Bible said to beat your swords into plowshares." It does say that, but the time to do that is when the Kingdom is established on the earth (see Isa. 2:4; Mic. 4:3). When Christ is ruling you can get rid of your sword, but until then you'd better keep your ammunition dry and you'd better be prepared. I do not agree that we should get rid of guns today. I think we need to protect our homes, our loved ones, and our nation. You and I are living in a big, bad world in which there are a lot of wild animals loose—they are human beings and they are two-legged, but they're mean and ferocious and they will destroy you. Also there are nations which are like that. In fact, that is the way God describes nations; He calls one a lion, another a bear, another a panther, and another a nondescript beast. Believe me, my friend, the nations of the world are like wild beasts, and we need to keep a few atomic bombs in our arsenal. Paul said, "For when they shall say, Peace and safety; then sudden destruction cometh upon them . . ." (1 Thess. 5:3). I am afraid we are going to have our teeth jarred out one of these days by the falling of a bomb, and we won't be able to retaliate because we have had too many soft-hearted and soft-headed leaders. The United Nations has as its motto the verse in Isaiah which says to beat your swords into plowshares; I think they ought to have this verse from Joel: "Beat your plowshares into swords." We need to be prepared today—we live in a bad, bad world.

Assemble yourselves, and come, all ye heathen, and gather yourselves together round about: thither cause thy mighty ones to come down, O LORD.

Let the heathen be wakened, and come up to the valley of Jehoshaphat: for there will I sit to judge all the heathen round about [Joel 3:11–12].

In the Olivet Discourse the Lord Jesus said that He will judge the nations and that He will judge them according to the way they have treated His people. Someone will ask, "Are they peculiar? Are they better?" No. Why, then, will He judge in this way? Because the 144,000 Jewish witnesses are going to be the only witnesses upon this earth after the church is removed. The Lord said that if anyone gave a cup of cold water in His name to one of these witnesses He would reward him. Many people think that that excuses them for giving only a dime or a quarter in the offering plate. However, may I say to you, in that day it would cost you your life to give a cup of cold water to one of the 144,000 who will be witnessing for Christ throughout the world.

> Put ye in the sickle, for the harvest is ripe: come, get you down; for the press is full, the vats overflow; for their wickedness is great [Joel 3:13].

When he speaks of a "harvest," he is speaking of the end of the age.

> Multitudes, multitudes in the valley of decision: for the day of the LORD is near in the valley of decision [Joel 3:14].

Joel identifies this period as "the day of the LORD." All that Joel says falls within the parentheses of the Day of the Lord which begins after the Rapture of the church with the Great Tribulation and continues through the second coming of Christ to establish His Kingdom and the judgment as to who will enter the Kingdom. Then Christ will reign for one thousand years; there will be a brief period of rebellion when Satan is let loose, then the final judgment at the Great White Throne, and eternity will begin. All of that is included in the Day of the Lord.

Again Joel speaks of the disturbance in the heavenly bodies—

> The sun and the moon shall be darkened, and the stars shall withdraw their shining.
>
> The LORD also shall roar out of Zion, and utter his voice from Jerusalem; and the heavens and the earth shall shake: but the LORD will be the hope of his people, and the strength of the children of Israel.
>
> So shall ye know that I am the LORD your God dwelling in Zion, my holy mountain: then shall Jerusalem be holy, and there shall no strangers pass through her any more [Joel 3:15-17].

Jerusalem is still being trodden down by Gentiles. The Garden Tomb was so crowded with tourists the last time we were there that we could not get into it. It was not Jews who were there, but it was Gentiles from all over the world—tourists coming and going all the time. The day is coming when the Garden Tomb will not be the tourist attraction in Jerusalem. Someday the Lord Himself will be there!

Now we move into the time of the Kingdom—

> **And it shall come to pass in that day, that the mountains shall drop down new wine, and the hills shall flow with milk, and all the rivers of Judah shall flow with waters, and a fountain shall come forth of the house of the LORD, and shall water the valley of Shittim [Joel 3:18].**

"And it shall come to pass in that day"—that is, the Day of the Lord. "The mountains shall drop down new wine"—this is in the time of the Kingdom. "And the hills shall flow with milk, and all the rivers of Judah shall flow with waters." Israel is short of water today, but they will not be short in that day.

"And a fountain shall come forth of the house of the LORD, and shall water the valley of Shittim." This is interesting because the valley of Shittim is on the other side of the Jordan River. How could these waters flow from Jerusalem across the Jordan? Zechariah tells us that the mountain will be split in that day. Instead of the great rift running from north of Byblos in Lebanon, down through the Sea of Galilee, through the Jordan valley, through the Dead Sea and into Africa, it is going to run the opposite direction—it is going to run east and west.

> **Egypt shall be a desolation, and Edom shall be a desolate wilderness, for the violence against the children of Judah, because they have shed innocent blood in their land [Joel 3:19].**

God will judge Egypt and Edom even into the millennial Kingdom. They have always been enemies of the nation Israel.

> **But Judah shall dwell for ever, and Jerusalem from generation to generation.**

For I will cleanse their blood that I have not cleansed: for the LORD dwelleth in Zion [Joel 3:20–21].

"For I will cleanse their blood that I have not cleansed"—the Lord has not yet moved in their behalf. "For the LORD dwelleth in Zion"—He doesn't dwell there today. Jerusalem is as pagan and heathen as any city on topside of the earth, but the day is coming when the Lord will dwell there. Then we will see all these things fulfilled. We would need to see Christ Himself there to say that these things are being fulfilled today. But that is not where we see Him, for at this very moment He is at God's right hand. It is my prayer that we might be continually conscious of Him and have the reality of His presence in our lives.

BIBLIOGRAPHY

(Recommended for Further Study)

Feinberg, Charles L. *The Minor Prophets*. Chicago, Illinois: Moody Press, 1976.

Gaebelein, Arno C. *The Annotated Bible*. 1917. Reprint. Neptune, New Jersey: Loizeaux Brothers, 1971.

Ironside, H. A. *The Minor Prophets*. Neptune, New Jersey: Loizeaux Brothers, n.d.

Jensen, Irving L. *Minor Prophets of Israel*. Chicago, Illinois: Moody Press, 1975.

Unger, Merrill F. *Unger's Commentary on the Old Testament*, Vol. 2. Chicago, Illinois: Moody Press, 1982.